The social history of Canada

MICHAEL BLISS, EDITOR

WITH AN INTRODUCTION BY ROBERT CRAIG BROWN

Rural life in Canada

ITS TREND AND TASKS

JOHN MACDOUGALL

UNIVERSITY OF TORONTO PRESS

© University of Toronto Press 1973

Toronto and Buffalo

Printed in Canada

ISBN (casebound) 0-8020-1885-8

ISBN (paperback) 0-8020-6145-1

Microfiche ISBN 0-8020-0225-0

LC 72-75735

The original edition of this work appeared in 1913

An introduction

BY ROBERT CRAIG BROWN

'Why is rural Ontario unable to keep the girls on the farm?' the *Globe* queried with alarm as 1911 drew to a close.[1] A few months later a Presbyterian minister urgently asked an audience at Geneva Park, Lake Couchiching; 'Have all of our women the vagrant heart?' (p. 40). Both the editorialist and the lecturer reflected a growing concern among Canadians after the publication of the 1911 census that Canada's rural life was in peril. Both knew that it was not just girls and women but boys and men too who were leaving farm homes and families by the dozens and the hundreds, especially in central Canada, for the excitement, the variety of social life, and the apparent prospect of a more prosperous life in the country's larger towns and cities.

If they were more worried about the girls than the boys, it was understandable enough. They were the foundations of Canada's families of the future. If they were more shocked by rural depopulation than by urban growth, that too seemed reasonable. In the city might be found 'a limited number of the leaders of to-day,' but from a vital countryside would come 'the empire-builders and founders of the kingdom of many to-morrows' (p. 213). 'There can be no health in the cities without corresponding health in the country,' the federal minister of agriculture observed in 1913. He told the House of Commons that it should aim at 'the creation of a rural civilization which will at once ensure a fuller and happier life to those in its midst, and prove a source and fount of strength to the State itself.'[2] W.C. Good, master of the Dominion Grange, was even more emphatic in his valedictory address to the Grange: 'It is admitted by all students of sociology that the country is the seedbed of the whole population. It therefore becomes a question of prime national importance to maintain the quality of this seedbed. If conditions are such as to cause the withdrawal of the best blood from the rural districts, or such as to favour the deterioration of rural life, the social and national disaster is imminent.'[3]

Rural Life in Canada is a vivid example of the public concern of Canadians over the impact of industrialization and urbanization upon Canada's farming population. The questions it poses and attempts to answer, and the social assumptions behind them, clearly reveal the nature of the anxiety of thoughtful citizens that the agricultural roots of their society were being eroded by the attractions of the new era. But *Rural Life in Canada* is also deliberately 'modern'; its structure is modelled upon what was thought to be the most progressive method of scientific analysis of society. The elaborate identification of the economic and social 'causes' of the rural problem, the cataloguing of the 'solutions' to it, and the careful outline of the particular role the investigating institution should play in reaching the 'solutions' are the essence of the 'social survey' technique adopted by both secular and religious reformers who combatted the social evils of the early twentieth century.

The 'problem' of rural life in Canada had not come about suddenly. The sons and daughters of Canada's farmers had always been attracted to the cities and towns. But since the implementation of the National Policy's protective tariff and the consequent growth of industrialization, the lure of apparently steady and rising wages[4] in urban factories and mills had intensified the steady movement away from the country. The increasing use of farm machinery in the last decades of the nineteenth century had lessened the farmer's dependence upon the labour of his offspring. By the end of the century western Canada was replacing Ontario as the major region for production of wheat for export and the McKinley tariff had closed the United States market for Ontario barley. All of these factors, and, most important, the growth of urban demands for agricultural products to feed the swelling city population, combined to force a revolution in central Canadian agriculture. Raising wheat and barley for export gave way to more intensive and more sophisticated mixed farming. Fruit and vegetable growing, stock raising and dairying, all generously encouraged by both the Ontario and Canadian governments, were well established before 1900. By 1911 an elaborate system of local and trunk line railways and a growing network of roads enabled the farmers quickly to despatch their meat, milk, cheese, butter, peas, and apples to city markets and just as quickly to receive back the ready-made clothes, furniture, pianos, and other consumer goods which reflected their changed life-style.

For those who accommodated to the 'new agriculture' of central Canada, life was prosperous in 1911. But the changeover was both expensive and demanding. Farmers who lacked the necessary capital or skills to adapt and those on marginal lands were driven out of the new home-dominated market. They went west to risk their luck in the exacting wheat farming of the prairies. They went to the United

States. And they went to Toronto and Montreal, to Sherbrooke and Hamilton, or to small regional industrial centres such as Midland and Collingwood. Even for those who did stay and did accommodate, all was not well. The increasing links with urban life were accompanied by a growing dependence upon the larger towns and cities. The small communities which had been essential service centres for local farmers became, at best, mere residential areas. Doctors and lawyers moved away, and tiny branch banks and one-room schools were closed in a general movement of consolidation of services in larger centres. The envy of urbanism and the threat to an older, more settled, rural way of life went hand-in-hand.

The Presbyterian Church in Canada was especially concerned with the social implications of the 'new agriculture' and, more parochially, its effect on the country church. For many years its Board of Moral and Social Reform and Evangelism had studied and worried about the host of complexities which it called 'The Problem of the City.' The board's report for 1911 was not encouraging. It was an open question whether Canada's cities would 'resemble the New Jerusalem or be typical of hell' but the prospects were dim. 'If things go for ten years more as they have gone for the past ten years, they will become either pagan or papal or worse.' It was unlikely that the city problem would be solved; perhaps the best that could be hoped for was that its worst evils would be tempered and its grossest hardships would be alleviated. One partial solution would be to stem the flow of population to the cities from the country. Indeed, an even more hopeful prospect was to induce city people to leave their corrupt surroundings for the regenerative environment of the countryside.

Rather late in the game the board turned its attention to the country — and assumed the romantic vision of rural living that was a classic cliché of the era; country life was pure, simple, and creative in ways that city life could never be.[5] But the board did recognize that the virus of urbanism was already infecting rural Canada, that the farming communities were already 'within the danger zone.' 'The cities seem likely in the near future to dominate the country,' it observed, 'and their rule will be ruinous if it is not righteous.'[6] In 1912 the board established a Summer School on the Country Church Problem at Lake Couchiching and asked John MacDougall, pastor of the Presbyterian Church in Spencerville, to prepare the series of lectures for the students.

John MacDougall was suited to the task. He was well educated and articulate, filled with missionary zeal, and long experienced with the problems of a rural pastorate. He had been born in Ormstown, Quebec, on 14 September 1859 and had attended the village school and then Huntingdon Academy. He had taken his Bachelor's degree at McGill with 'highest honours in philosophy' and the gold medal in English, graduating in 1886. For the next three years MacDougall attended Presbyterian College in Montreal and was one of the founders of the Student Volunteer Movement. After graduation, ordination, and marriage, MacDougall and his young bride left in the summer of 1889 for the newly established mission field in North Honan, China. Mrs MacDougall's illness forced the couple's return to Canada in 1893 and MacDougall began his long career of service to rural Presbyterians. He had been moderator of the Synod of Montreal and Ottawa in 1912 and at various times served on a number of the boards of the General Assembly which reflected his interests and special competence.[7]

Publication of his Geneva Park lectures as *Rural Life in Canada: Its Trend and Tasks* brought him brief fame as 'a pioneer in the study of rural life' and invitations to speak at the Presbyterian Church's Pre-Assembly Congress in 1913 and at the Social Service Congress in Ottawa in 1914 as well as an honorary doctoral degree from Queen's University. The Great War overtook both the 'rural problem' and MacDougall's claim to public attention and claimed the life of a son, one of the MacDougalls' six children. John MacDougall returned to his rural pastorates in Ontario, retired in 1929, and died on 27 November 1939. His friend and pastor in his retirement years, Reverend Ernest Long, noted that John Mac-Dougall was 'a good theologian, a keen Biblical scholar and an authority on Canadian poetry.' *Rural Life in Canada,* Long recalled, 'earned him wide recognition throughout the continent.'[8]

The Geneva Park lectures, which became the first six chapters of *Rural Life in Canada,* were such a success that the Board of Social Service and Evangelism[9] asked MacDougall to repeat them at Pine Hill College in Halifax and Knox College in Toronto during the 1912 fall term. For the occasion MacDougall added a seventh lecture, a missionary call to his student pastors, 'Students for the Ministry and the Rural Problem.' The final chapter, 'Rural Uplift Elsewhere,' may have been in the original Geneva Park series but probably was added later to round out the book for publication. 'Thorough-going and orderly,' 'analytic, critical and constructive,' 'it can hardly be too heartily commended,' were the comments of the *Presbyterian* after the publication of *Rural Life in Canada*. The church, said the paper, 'without departing from her true mission, can lend a hand to beautify and ennoble country life, to enlarge its horizon and make it more attractive. Mr. MacDougall drafts in outline a programme of service for the Country Church which shows how broad a field of usefulness lies open here. That special training is needed for leadership in such a work goes without saying. There is a call for strong men to prepare for and dedicate themselves to the permanent rural pastorate.'[10]

Rural Life in Canada was indeed 'a call.' The Board of Social Service and Evangelism thought that it would 'give rise to keen interest in this urgent problem.' For the board itself, MacDougall's book was not the final answer; rather, it identified the source and pointed towards the solution of the rural problem: 'The modern industrial development leading to the concentration of population in large cities and towns, and the migration movements drawing men and women away from the older settled parts to occupy the vast open stretches of Canada, have given rise to a situation that has created many problems for the country church. During the last few years the situation has become acute and has given rise to a demand for a thorough investigation of the whole problem.'[11] During the next year, in co-operation with the equally concerned Methodist Church, 'social surveys' were carried out in a small number of rural and urban areas.[12]

The Great War forced the Presbyterian Church to slacken its assault on the problems of rural life in Canada. But the impact of the war on the countryside – the steep increases in prices of agricultural products and in costs of production, the elaborate drives for greater productivity, and the growing urgency of the shortage of farm labour, heightened by the anticipation of the introduction of conscription – intensified the difficulties of rural life. The church, fully alive to the social dislocations of the war, quickened its conscience and sharpened its vision of the causes of rural unrest. In *Rural Life in Canada* MacDougall carefully outlined the economic woes of Canada's farmers. But even with the hoary evils of land speculation, transport monopolies, trade restraints, and wastage of resources, he asserted that the economic plight of agriculturalists was self-imposed, not the result of some intrinsic flaw in the economic system. It was not a problem in trade but a problem of attitude; the farmers had failed to keep up with the increasing economic complexity of their livelihood. As he put it, 'the solution is not economic in nature, but ethical — it depends not on knowledge, but character' (p. 107). Whether living out the war years in rural Ontario charges changed MacDougall's ideas is not known. The church itself still believed that 'the greatest force in enriching of rural life must be spiritual.' But by 1917 it was ready to assert that the chief reason for rural discontent was not moral laxity but the economic system. The selfishness, the greed, the materialism of Canadian farmers was the product of their economic environment. 'The main cause of depletion and impoverishment of rural Canada is economic,' the board reported to the General Assembly. 'Hence economic forces will have their due place in the repopulation and re-enrichment of the country.'[13]

MacDougall's 'pioneering' effort in rural sociology is scarcely original in either ideas or analysis. Rather, it is a clear and able synthesis of the work of others. As its references and examples amply indicate, both the identification of and the solution to the problem draw heavily upon the 1909 report of the Country Life Commission in the United States,[14] the investigations of the Federal Council of Churches of Christ in America, and the efforts of James W. Robertson and the Commission of Conservation in Canada. By singling out character defects as the root cause of his social problem, MacDougall was echoing the accepted wisdom of his day. Few Canadians and even fewer Canadian churchmen were ready to argue that the social malaise of the countryside had its origins in the institutions of rural society rather than in its members. MacDougall's solution followed naturally enough and was as old as the church itself: 'Christ calls strong men to heathendom through the prospect of uplifting a pagan people. Does He not,' he asked, 'also call such men to the country through the prospect of upholding a Christian one?' (p. 212).

The basic threat to the Canadian countryside was that its Protestant moral order was being undermined — MacDougall all too easily assumed that what he thought was happening in rural Ontario and his native Eastern Townships could be generalized into the total

Canadian rural experience. It was challenged by French Canadians[15] and by immigrants,[16] who were displacing the original settlers at an alarming rate. The church could not stop French Canadians and immigrants from occupying abandoned farms or settling new ones; though, of course, by making life more attractive and more meaningful for the original settlers, it could reduce the incentives for them to leave or sell their lands. And a strong and dedicated rural clergy could minister to the 'foreigners' who did come, could lead them to 'the greater freedom and the higher ideals of the Reformed religion.'

But the greater problem was with the 'Canadian stock' who remained in rural Canada. 'Modern industrial society,' 'the real cause of the present rural problem,' had sapped their co-operative instincts, had corroded their spiritual values, had undermined their dedication to the Christian life. True, the new agriculture was 'richer by far in potentialities of social satisfaction through collaboration' (p. 133) than had been the pioneer drudgery of the past. Specialization, organization, conservation, the adoption of the most advanced scientific techniques and of the principles of economic co-operation were essential to the survival of rural Canada. The problem was that the farmers had grasped only at the superficialities of the opportunity held out to them, had failed to comprehend the full value promised by the myriad organizations and agencies who promoted the 'new agriculture,' had plunged into ruthless and destructive competition, and had forsaken their social conscience for acquisitiveness and greed. For rural churchmen the task was all too apparent: to lead the farmers to embrace the 'new responsibilities' that accompanied the rewards of the 'new agriculture.' Only then would agriculturists approach their calling 'with a new sense of personal worth and of service rendered' (p. 148). The demands upon the churchmen would be great. They would need to be specially trained and doubly dedicated to service in rural pastorates. But their function was what it always had been, to instill and maintain the moral foundations of a Christian society in a rapidly changing secular world.

Rural Life in Canada, then, is an interesting period piece in Canadian social history. It vividly reflects the social assumptions, values, prejudices, and aspirations of John MacDougall and his generation. The casual marshalling of apparently compelling statistics and the popular rhetoric of social science methodology and modernism give the book a veneer of freshness that may well have enhanced its appeal but could not disguise its traditional analysis. That social analysis was collective only in so far as the rural problem was the aggregate of the moral backsliding of the individual members of the rural community. The social remedy was institutional only in so far as the established institutions of society — the home, the school, and the church — were called upon to rededicate themselves to the moral betterment of the individuals they served. Careful study of the rural life problem ultimately came down to this. Should the church 'teach men here how to grow better cabbages?' MacDougall asked. 'She need not. But she should teach men everywhere and always that it is their duty to grow better cabbages ... it is for the church to deal with the moral prerequisites of better husbandry, and hold out the better resultant life as an incentive' (p. 181).

NOTES

Rural Life in Canada: Its Trend and Tasks was originally published in Toronto in 1913 by the Westminster Company, Limited, for the Board of Special Service and Evangelism, The Presbyterian Church in Canada. The writer of the original Introduction, James W. Robertson, C.M.G., D.Sc., LL.D., was a member of the Commission of Conservation and also chairman of the Royal Commission on Industrial Training and Technical Education.

1 Globe, Toronto, 23 Dec. 1911; cited in J.C. Hopkins, ed., *The Canadian Annual Review of Public Affairs, 1911* (Toronto, 1912), p. 399.
2 *Can. H. of C. Debates,* 24 Jan. 1913.
3 *Farmer Citizen: My Fifty Years in the Canadian Farmers' Movement* (Toronto, 1958), p. 94.
4 See Canada, *Royal Commission on the Relations of Labor and Capital in Canada,* 1889. An edited digest of the report and the testimony, *Canada Investigates Industrialism: The Royal Commission on the Relations of Labor and Capital, 1889,* by Greg Kealey, is to be published in this series.
5 Even James W. Robertson, the nation's leading agricultural educationalist, embraced the romantic vision of rural life: 'Farming is gathering sunshine, forging wealth out of chaos, — gathering and humanizing into wealth for the service of the race the great unused

power of nature,' he observed to his fellow members of the Commission of Conservation (see *infra*, p. 14).

6 United Church of Canada Archives (UCCA), *Presbyterian Church in
Canada, General Assembly, 1910-1911,* Annual Report, Board of
Moral and Social Reform and Evangelism, 1911, pp. 267-72.

7 Boards of French Evangelization, Foreign Missions, and Young
Peoples' Societies.

8 UCCA, Biographical file, John MacDougall, *United Church Observer,*
1 Feb. 1940, Obituary by E.E.L. (Reverend Ernest E. Long), p. 27.

9 The board's name was changed in 1912.

10 17 July 1913, p. 53. The *Westminster,* another unofficial church
publication, perversely failed to note the publication of Mac-
Dougall's book. In the spring of 1913 it published a series of articles
by John A. Cormie on the problems of country churches, largely
inspired by the report of the Country Life Commission in the United
States in 1909. On the histories of these and other church publications, see E.A. Christie, 'The Presbyterian Church in Canada and Its
Official Attitude toward Public Affairs and Social Problems,
1875-1925,' MA thesis, University of Toronto, 1955, pp. 308-12.

11 UCCA, *Presbyterian Church in Canada, General Assembly,
1912-1913,* Annual Report, Board of Social Service and Evangelism,
1913, pp. 291-2.

12 Christie, 'The Presbyterian Church in Canada,' pp. 40-1, and Richard
Allen, *The Social Passion: Religion and Social Reform in Canada,
1914-28* (Toronto, 1971), p. 25.

13 Cited in Christie, 'The Presbyterian Church in Canada,' p. 42.

14 For a brief summary, see Carl N. Degler, *Out of Our Past* (New
York, 1959), pp. 342-9.

15 *Infra,* pp. 32-6. The Board of French Evangelization of the Presbyterian Church in Canada, upon which MacDougall had served, reported in 1912 that: 'Evidence is abundant of the consistent and
persistent purpose of the Church of Rome to use every agency
available for her own aggrandizement. From her viewpoint in so
doing she is advancing the Kingdom of God. Whatever restraint may
be laid on her politically, the great deliverance must come from the
growth of French Protestantism; so leading the Roman Catholic laity
in particular to an appreciation of the greater freedom and the
higher ideals of the Reformed religion. The other provinces cannot
afford to be indifferent to what happens in Quebec. If they are they

will sooner or later realize that the health of the whole body
depends upon the health of every part of it.' *General Assembly,
1912-1913*, Report, p. 60.
16 *Infra,* pp. 45-6. Likewise, at the 1912 General Assembly, the Home
Mission Committee (Western Section) noted that: 'This rapidly
increasing population must be provided with the means of grace. The
strangers must be reached for their own sake, for the sake of Canada.
"You can find the Heathen nearer" is now literally true. Foreigners
are crowding about our doors. We may not overlook the opportunity
that has been afforded us of ministering to those who are coming to
our shores' (p. 4).

FURTHER READING

Scant attention has been paid by historians to the problem sketched
out in *Rural Life in Canada.* Richard Allen's *The Social Passion*
(Toronto, 1971) puts it in the context of the churches' more general
social concerns, as do E.A. Christie, 'The Presbyterian Church in
Canada and Its Official Attitude toward Public Affairs and Social
Problems, 1875-1925,' MA thesis, University of Toronto, 1955, and
M.V. Royce, 'The Contribution of the Methodist Church to Social
Welfare in Canada,' MA thesis, University of Toronto, 1940.
MacDougall's brief addresses to the Pre-Assembly Congress and the
Social Service Congress may be found in *Pre-Assembly Congress of
the Presbyterian Church in Canada* (Toronto, 1913), and Social
Service Council of Canada, *The Social Service Congress of Canada,
1914* (Toronto, 1914). Of the great amount of contemporary
supplementary material on the 'rural problem,' the reports of the
Lands Committee of the Commission of Conservation, *Annual
Reports, 1911-1921,* are especially interesting. Many of the sections
on agriculture in A. Shortt and A.G. Doughty, eds., *Canada and Its
Provinces* (Toronto, 1913-14), are useful. See especially J.A.
Ruddick, 'National Aid to the Farm,' in volume 11, pp. 651-77,
and C.C. James, 'History of Farming,' in volume 18, pp. 551-82.
Valuable statistical information on contemporary agriculture may
be found in M.C. Urquhart and K.A. Buckley, eds., *Historical
Statistics of Canada* (Toronto, 1965), section L. Two interesting

SHEEP HUSBANDRY IN BRITISH COLUMBIA.

"There are no heathen oaks, no Gentile pines,
The soil beneath our feet is Christian soil."

Here's to the land of the rock and the pine,
   Here's to the land of the raft and the river,
Here's to the land where the sunbeams shine,
   And the night that is bright with the north-light's quiver!

Here's to the land with its blanket of snow—
   To the hero and hunter the welcomest pillow;
Here's to the land where the storm-winds blow
   Three days ere the mountains can talk to the billow!

Here's to the land of the axe and the plow,
   Here's to the hearties that give them their glory,—
With stroke upon stroke and with blow upon blow
   The might of the forest has passed into story!

Here's to her hills of the moose and the deer,
   Here's to her forests, her fields and her flowers,
Here's to her homes of unchangeable cheer,
   And the maid 'neath the shade of her own native bowers!

Here's to the buckwheats that smoke on her board,
   Here's to the maple that sweetens their story,
Here's to the scythe that we swing like a sword,
   And here's to the fields where we gather our glory!

              —*William Wye Smith.*

PREFACE

THIS volume is the outcome of a request from the Board of Social Service of the Presbyterian Church in Canada to the writer to prepare a short course of lectures dealing with the problem of the Country Church, for the Summer School at Geneva Park, on Lake Couchiching.

Under the direction of the Board the lectures were again delivered in the Presbyterian College, Halifax, and in Knox College, Toronto. The seventh chapter represents an additional lecture to the students of these colleges.

In compliance with the desire of the Board the lectures, in somewhat enlarged form, are now brought before the public. The manner of its production accounts for the use of the direct address and other features in the form of the volume.

Although the incidental illustrations have been drawn from a local field, and the situation in Ontario is most in evidence, and although one particular branch of the Church is occasionally referred to, the viewpoint of the book is national.

The writer begs that the volume will be regarded by no one as a treatise on its subject. It is put forth as but a series of individual impressions upon an important problem in national welfare.

SPENCERVILLE, ONTARIO,
28th February, 1913.

Where are the men of my heart's desire?
  Of the British blood and the loyal names?
Some are north, at the home hearth-fire,
  Where the hemlock glooms and the maple flames;
And some are tramping the old world round
For the pot of gold they have never found!
                                    —*Theodore Roberts.*

CONTENTS

CHAPTER V.

Theology and sociology alike requisite. The establishing of the Kingdom of God affords the requisite standpoint. The course of the Providence of God and the Spirit of God in the trend of the age bestows the requisite insight whereby to discern her function. Two factors in the founding of the Kingdom—the salvation of souls and the redemption of society. Two factors found in the trend of the age—social service and preventive work. The church, how far institutional?

CHAPTER VI.

Executive oversight. The rural survey. Church union or federation. Special preparation for the ministry. Direct ministry of teaching. Utilization of established agencies. Of new agencies.

CHAPTER VII.

Students to-day possessed of the spirit of social service. Social science not sufficiently taught. An imperative call for such teaching. Equality in status in rural ministry and urban. The country ministry a call to strong men. The permanent rural pastorate. Training for the country ministry.

CHAPTER VIII.

The labors of John Frederick Oberlin. Rural reconstruction in Denmark. Advance in Ireland through co-operation. The rural life movement in the United States. The challenge to the Christian Church.

ILLUSTRATIONS

O London holds the hearts of men,
  And London's paved with gold;
But ah, to hear the lark again,
  And see the buds unfold!

O London stole my youth away
  The while she gave me bread;
She killed my soul from day to day,
  And gave me gold instead.

But in the twilight cold and gray,
  Above the city's voice
I hear the mowers mow the hay,
  I hear the birds rejoice.

              —*J. A. Middleton, "Exile."*

INTRODUCTION

We are just beginning to realize that our vast areas of good lands could and should carry happy homes for millions more people and not have them huddled into big towns where the children cannot play. How stupid the people are who are rich and strong and do not give the children a chance! Inexpressibly stupid, no matter how they may pride themselves on motor cars and big ships and fine buildings, if the children of the poor as well as the rich have no chance to play on the grass and pick flowers and drink in the enriching vigor of good air. Such people do not match our land. They are like a degenerate, of an old ancestral stock, that was once strong before luxury and self-indulgence and all kinds of libertine behavior made him a despicable thing. As I have gone over this continent I have wondered when the man shall arise who will say, " The Lord expects that these plains and mountains and forests and orchards will be occupied by people to reflect His image and match the setting of their homes."

Let us consider the conservation of the resources of the land; not only to grow big crops, to increase the exports and make the balances of trade stand out with startling figures, but to have a better boy, to have a more beautiful girl, that the next generation for whom we are trustees should still more reflect back the grandeur of human life and have a fair chance to give

13

expression to it through the wise use of our natural resources. Farming is gathering sunshine, forging wealth out of chaos,—gathering and humanizing into wealth for the service of the race the great unused powers of nature. It is one of the great fundamental occupations, and therefore the interests of the men who follow it are worth conserving. We have laid out our school system—that is, our rural public schools that we boast so much about—to train a boy to read and write and figure as the essential means of conserving and training for use his God-given powers and obligations to gather sunshine. Maybe the preparation does not qualify for the job, and the boy goes to town where he will find some job to suit his training.

Why has the Young Men's Christian Association gone on faster and more widely than some other organizations? It is not attempting to save men's souls apart from their bodies; it is not attempting to help men by appealing to their intellect only. By inclusion of the body, mind and spirit, with training for his occupation, the whole man may be saved into faith in a Christ who, as the perfect example, was Himself trained that way.

And when we men who are responsible have done these things then we shall still be unprofitable servants; because no man can achieve more than a fraction of the service that will pay for what he came into, all unearned by his own labor or life. I wish the churches out in the rural districts ever-abounding success in making these things known to the youth—God's partner in the new earth; that it is worth while to be consciously a partner in the care of old Mother Earth, as a home for the race, bearing fine crops, with weeds suppressed, diseases and vile things under the restraining control of intelligent, educated man, and Earth herself becoming more beautiful and fertile; that, when he is far enough on to see and hope for the new heaven and the new earth wherein dwelleth righteousness, he has no real gain from the vision unless he takes his part in making the earth new and righteous where he lives; and that he best gives expression to his life, as one of the partners, who helps to reveal and reflect God through his labor and his love.

JAMES W. ROBERTSON.

HASTINGS COUNTY, ONTARIO, LOSING 3,138 IN RURAL POPULATION IN A DECADE.

"Oh, why should Canada's children roam?"

DEPLETION OF RURAL POPULATION

How tame now seems to me this herdsman life,
Unprofitable too; naught do I here,—
Naught that can serve good purpose. Why then stay?
Others could tend these herds as well as I,
And haply better, for my thoughts are far
From meads and kine and all the servile round
Of household duties, the same from year to year,
Far from the rural dull routine. .   .   .
                    —*Charles Heavysege, " Saul."*

Rural Life in Canada

CHAPTER I.

DEPLETION OF RURAL POPULATION.

" The Poetic Genius of my country found me—as the prophetic bard Elijah did Elisha—at the plough, and threw her inspiring mantle over me. She bade me sing the loves, the joys, the rural scenes and pleasures of my native soil in my native tongue; I tuned my wild artless notes as she inspired." So wrote Robert Burns. That he was bred to the plow gave Burns his knowledge of rural life; his genius gave him insight into its significance. And thus in the poem which made the Plowman's fame, and in its most impassioned part, the patriot-poet prays:

O Scotia, my dear, my native soil!
For whom my warmest wish to Heaven is sent,
Long may thy hardy sons of rustic toil
Be blest with health and peace and sweet content.
And oh! may Heaven their simple lives prevent
From luxury's contagion, weak and vile.
Then, howe'er crowns and coronets be rent,
A virtuous populace may rise the while,
And stand, a wall of fire, around their much-loved Isle!

The welfare of this " wall of fire " is fundamental in national well-being.

" Agriculture," says that keen-visioned watchman on

the towers, Dr. James W. Robertson, in a masterly plea
for the conservation of our agricultural resources, " is
not only an occupation which some individuals follow
for profit: it is a great national interest determining
in a dominant way the fortunes of this nation and the
opportunities and the character of the population.   So,
while the improving of Canadian agriculture primarily
concerns the farmer and his family, it affects the status
of Canada, its outlook and its destiny."*   Any widespread movement or persistent tendency which affects
the status of the rural population is therefore a matter
of concern to all, whether dwelling in city or in
country, who have at heart the national welfare,
and consequently sets a task for the Home, the School,
the State, and the Church.   Such a problem is given
by the changing relations of city and country life.   The
rapid growth of urban population in comparison with
rural is a phenomenon so pronounced, so widespread,
and so persistent as to arrest universal attention.

The report of the Board of Social Service presented
to the General Assembly of the Presbyterian Church in
Canada in 1911 called that church's attention with
emphatic force to the problem of the city.   That report
was an outcome of a two years' study of the situation—
a study not only of the down-town problem, but of the
up-town problem as well; not only of the congested
centre, but also of the suburb.   It stated in terse terms
that the problem exists; asserted that in Canada it is
just emerging as one of the most urgent of national
questions; and claimed that it is THE problem of the
twentieth century.   A fuller study of the situation

* Commission of Conservation, Canada, III, p. 89.

reveals that we have as vital and as urgent a problem
of the country as of the city.   It is the counterpart and
correlative of the city problem.   And though its moral
outcrop is not so immediately obvious as in the case of
the city, it is in its ultimate issues the more fundamental of the two.

We shall consider in our first chapter the depletion
of rural life in three of its dimensions, physical, social,
and moral, as seen in the numerical decline in population, the social strain upon the home and all the institutions of society, and the moral dangers incident to the
situation.

The first or physical dimension, numerical decrease,
is found throughout large districts of country.   Let us
glance first at some local illustrations.

Within a recent seven-year period seventy-six young
persons left my pastoral charge for the cities or the
West.   A good proportion were from among our best
church workers.   They were not lost to the cause.
One, for instance, trained in Christian work in the
Young People's Guild at Spencerville, was the means
of founding two congregations at Francis and its vicinity, in Saskatchewan.   They were not lost to the cause,
but what did their removal not mean to the church in
Spencerville?

Some few years ago a young Spencerville farmer said
to me, " When my father bought out the land we are
now working he displaced thirty-eight persons.   We are
four, with four constant hired help."   The change has
meant no economic loss.   While we were conversing
he was on his way to Montreal in charge of two carloads
of stall-fed cattle for the British market, all from his
father's barns.   Farming had improved under con-

solidation, but what of the social loss where eight persons replaced thirty-eight?

There is one school district within the bounds of my congregation where for four years past there have been but three children on the roll, and for three months of the last school year but one pupil was in attendance. Yet the school registers of forty years ago show an average attendance of forty-five pupils. What is the social significance of this fact?

Spencerville, a hamlet of two hundred inhabitants, is situated on the Nation River between two concession roads. On the nearer of these concessions, right over against the village, are seven consecutive farms, once occupied, now without an occupant. What is the sociological bearing of this circumstance?

These incidents of the situation—these indications of a process of change—might be duplicated with variation in form or degree from the experience of every observer. They are evidences of a universal tendency, a world-movement. Population the world over is massing itself in cities. Cities are becoming congested, the country depleted.

Canada during the last decennial census period increased in population by 1,833,523, yet her rural growth was only 574,878, while her urban expansion was 1,258,645. She added 34.13 per cent. to her total population during the decade, but only 17.16 to her people in the country, though 62.25 to those in town and city. We are apt to think of the prairies as purely agricultural regions, yet Saskatchewan, adding 389 per cent. to her rural population, added 648 per cent. to her urban population; and Alberta, increasing by 344 per cent. in rural growth, increased by 588 per cent. in urban growth.

British Columbia gained 100,318 in rural, but 113,505 in urban, population in the decade. Manitoba, rich in still unoccupied land, won 70,511 for her farms and hamlets, but 129,892 for her villages, towns and cities. Quebec, although so largely agricultural, gained 39,951 in country population while advancing by 313,863 in city growth.

Our country people formed, when the previous census was taken in 1901, 62.4 per cent. of the total population; when the recent one was taken in 1911 they had fallen to 54.4 per cent. Our city population, 37.6 in 1901, had grown to 45.6 in 1911.

The proportion of rural to total population has fallen in every Province during the decade; in Prince Edward Island from 85 per cent. to 84; in Saskatchewan from 80 to 73 per cent.; in New Brunswick from 76 per cent. to 71; in Manitoba from 72 to 56 per cent.; from 71 per cent. to 62 in Nova Scotia and in Alberta; from 60 to 51 per cent. in Quebec; in Ontario from 57 per cent. to 47; and in British Columbia from 49 to 48 per cent.

But it is not from relative increase merely, of city as compared with country, that the grave rural situation arises. Our addition of 34 per cent. in a decade does indeed present serious problems of several kinds, in evangelization, in assimilation, and even in transportation. But it does not give rise to the rural problem. Nor does the fact that we added 62 per cent. to the city and but 17 to the country population reveal the real heart of the problem. The country's loss is not relative merely, but absolute. The question is not one of slackened growth, but of waste begun. The country is not simply falling behind in the upward race; she is not even standing still; she is slipping downhill again and knows not how to stay her course.

We did not complete our survey of the Provinces a moment ago. We ceased with Quebec, whose gain as there given in figures we now notice was equal to 4 per cent. in her rural parishes, but 48 per cent. in her industrial centres. We have yet to consider that while New Brunswick had an accession of 22,262 to the inhabitants of her cities she suffered a diminution of 1,493 in her residents in the country; while Prince Edward Island towns simply maintained their ground, her townships fell back by some 9,546; while Nova Scotia's cities gained to the extent of 56,745 her farming districts lost by some 23,981; and that Ontario, adding 392,511 inhabitants to her cities and towns, parted with 52,184 from her rural homes.

Let us look more particularly at Ontario's loss. Grenville, the county in which Spencerville is situated, had 21,021 people in 1901; now it has 17,545. Stormont numbered 27,042 a decade ago, but to-day 24,775. North Lanark by the previous census was credited with 17,236, by the recent one with 14,624. Frontenac, having then 24,746, now numbers 21,944. Lennox and Addington eleven years ago were given 23,346, one year ago 20,386. East Hastings, from 27,943 had fallen off to 24,978. Lambton East from 26,219 had dwindled to 22,223; North Bruce from 27,424 had diminished to 23,783.

Looking at other counties from another angle, we find that North Wellington lost 14.6 per cent. in the decade; East Huron decreased 15.2 per cent. during the ten years; Dufferin's population diminished by 15.6 in the same period; North Middlesex fell away by 16.3;

Grenville parted with 16.6 per cent. of her people, but was outclassed by South Bruce with a loss of 16.9 per cent. These three last-named counties saw just one-sixth of their population leave their bounds within the ten-year period.

But the loss is heavier still. These figures are for counties. The statistics for the counties include those for the towns. Now, with some few exceptions, such as Deseronto, with a loss of 42.9 per cent., Graven-hurst, of 24.3, or Almonte, of 18.9, the towns are holding their own. Consequently the percentage of loss is still higher for the townships than for the counties. Let us look at a few illustrative examples. Grenville lost 16.6 per cent., but her rural loss was 18.6 per cent., and the township of Edwardsburg, of which Spencerville is the centre, lost 21 per cent. The apparent loss in South Bruce is 16.9 per cent.; the real rural loss 19.3 per cent., and the actual loss in Kinloss township 23 per cent. The census informs us that Dufferin was a loser by 15.6 per cent.; the rural exodus was 18.5; but Gara-fraxa decreased 24 per cent. In North Bruce the rural loss was 18.2 per cent.; in East Grey and in East Lambton 18.9 per cent.; in South Grey 20.4 per cent., and in West Elgin 21.6 per cent. But what shall we say of such a case as that of North Grey, whose rural loss was 21.9 per cent. while her total gain was 7.8 per cent.; whose townships of Keppel and Sarawak decreased by 34.3 and 48 per cent., while her urban population, in the towns of Owen Sound and Meaford and the village of Shallow Lake, increased by 48.5 per cent.? Or of Peterborough West, adding 20 per cent to the total population, and 29 per cent. to her city of Peterborough, but losing 51.5 per cent. from her township of Galway?

When the situation in Ontario is thoroughly canvassed we find that of the 526 townships in Ontario, exclusive of the immigration area—Algoma, Nipissing, Thunder Bay, and Rainy River—there has been a decrease of population in 423; and that of the 75 census districts containing rural as well as urban population, 60 suffered decrease in their rural population. If, again, we except the five districts in the New North, we find that in ten districts only is there growth of rural population.

We may perhaps realize the contrast more vividly still by placing rural loss over against urban gain in certain counties. Carlton lost 2,561 in rural population and gained 6,587 in urban; in Elgin the respective loss and gain were 3,302 and 4,128; in Grey, 10,782 and 7,083; in Haldimand 1,139 and 1,468; in West Hastings, 1,586 and 1,063; in Kent, 2,701 and 1,502. West Lambton's rural loss of 2,594 stands over against an urban gain of 1,980; South Lanark's loss of 1,460 over against a gain of 1,215. Leeds suffered a rural loss of 2,150, but with an offset in urban gain of 1,118; Ontario—the county of that name—met with a rural loss of 2,091, but had an urban increase of 2,689; in Parry Sound the respective loss and gain were 1,970 and 3,581; in Perth, 3,792 and 3,013; in Renfrew, 2,724 and 1,961. Russell lost 1,204 in rural population; Wellington, 4,189; and Simcoe, 5,431 while gaining respectively 5,472, 3,035, and 5,472 in urban growth.

The census summary informs us that the rural decrease in Ontario is 52,184. This is 4.19 per cent. But the rural gain in the five new districts is 44,940. Therefore the rural loss in Old Ontario was 97,124, or 8.36 per cent. And the rural gain in the ten growing

IN PICTOU COUNTY, NOVA SCOTIA, LOSING 26.5 PER CENT. IN A DECADE.

Is Acadia Arcadia no more?

districts was 12,545. Therefore the rural loss in the sixty waning census districts is 109,669, or 10.82 per cent.

Yet Ontario, with a net increase of 1.5 per cent. per annum through the excess of births over deaths, would have gained 200,183 in rural population in the decade. Moreover, fully 404,000 immigrants gave, at the ports of entry, Ontario as their destination, and of these fully 30 per cent. gave farming as their occupation. From this additional source the Province received an increase of rural population amounting to 121,200, without considering natural increase. The migration from her farms therefore amounts not to 52,184, but 373,567.

Nova Scotia's loss of 23,981 amounts to 7 per cent.; and the decrease is found in every district except two; in these the rural growth amounts to only seven-tenths of one per cent. In several counties the decline is severe; Colchester, 10.5 per cent.; Inverness, 11.9; Shelburne and Queen's, 14.8; North Cape Breton and Victoria, 15.8; Pictou, 26.6. The urban growth in Pictou, on the other hand, is 72 per cent. Severe as is this loss sustained by the counties, the townships in this case again alone reveal the real facts. The counties might be taken in almost unbroken succession to exhibit cases of severe declension in special townships. Advocate in Cumberland, for instance, loses 40 per cent.

In Prince Edward Island the diminution amounts to 10.8 per cent. and is general throughout the Island. In parts it is severe. In King's County, for instance, Township No. 40 loses 36 per cent.; in Queen's County, Township No. 20 loses 37 per cent.

In New Brunswick, because of expansion into new areas the loss is slighter, yet even here there is a loss in more than half the counties. In Westmoreland the falling off is 13 per cent.; in Charlotte, 13; in King's and Albert, 17. The loss in townships is startling. Hampton, in King's, loses 40 per cent.; Hillsborough, in Albert, 41; Sussex, in King's, 45; Madawaska and St. Francis, in Victoria, 47 and 53 respectively.

In Quebec, though there is a rural gain amounting over the whole Province to 4 per cent., yet there is a shrinkage in twenty-seven counties; in some severe: Montmorency, for instance, meets with a loss of 11.7 per cent.; Chambly and Vercheres, 11.9; Yamaska, 12; Richelieu, 20.2; and Laval, 23.7 per cent.

The contrast between rural loss and urban gain in certain counties is as vivid in other Provinces as in the case of Ontario. King's County, Prince Edward Island, lost 3,178 in rural population while gaining 1,089 in urban. In Nova Scotia the respective loss and gain were: in Cape Breton, South, 1,173 and 19,438; in Cumberland, 1,713 and 6,088; in Inverness 2,630 and 3,848; in Pictou, 5,885 and 8,284; in Shelburne and Queen's, 3,329 and 3,112; and in Yarmouth, 1,211 and 1,562. Charlotte, in New Brunswick, lost 2,999 in rural population and gained 1,713 in urban, while in King's and Albert the loss and gain were 5,666 and 3,371, and in Westmoreland, 4,319 and 6,880.

In Manitoba the receding of the tide has just set in. Lisgar records a loss of 7.5 per cent.; a score of districts show recession. Were it not for expansion over new territory towards the north, the whole Province would show decline in rural population.

Assuming that the natural increase of population is 1.5 per cent. per annum, the rural population of the Dominion in 1901, 3,349,516, should have increased by 547,878 before the census was taken in 1911. Of the 1,715,326 immigrants who came to Canada during the decade, approximately one-third at the ports of entry gave farming as their occupation. These, with the same annual rate of increase, give a further augment of 670,258. The rural population thus received an accretion of 1,218,136. The actual growth was 574,878. Therefore 643,258 persons left our country districts during the decade. That all of these are not found in our Canadian cities does not alter the facts of the case.

> On soft Pacific slopes,—beside
> Strange floods that northward rave and fall—
> Where chafes Acadia's chainless tide,
> Thy sons await thy call.
> They wait; but some in exile—some
> With strangers housed, in stranger lands. . . . .*

Winnipeg is not the third Canadian city, if we count by Canadian-born population; Boston is; 200,000 of her people are Canadian. There are several New England cities with a majority of their population Canadian born. When the figures of the Census Bureau were published a year ago, men asked in perplexity, "Where is the other million?" The Canadian nurses serving in American hospitals might be given as the first count in the answer. Canada set about making of herself a good place for manufacturers, and succeeded, but at the cost of becoming a less desirable

* Charles G. D. Roberts, " In Divers Tones."

place for farmers. Her manufacturers would in due
time have arisen, because of her advantages, and would
have been in an immensely stronger position eventually
with a broader agricultural base.

Such is the record for a single decade. We must
not, because of space, go into similar detail in regard to
earlier periods. We should expect to find that in each
decade the proportion of rural population grew less,
and such is the case. We note the preceding one only.
Between 1891 and 1901 the rural population of Prince
Edward Island fell from 87 per cent. to 85; of New
Brunswick, from 84 to 76; of Nova Scotia, from 82 to
71; of Manitoba, from 73 to 72; of Quebec, from 66 to
60; of Ontario, from 61 to 57, and of British Columbia,
from 62 to 49; while throughout the Dominion the fall
was from 72.3 per cent. to 62.4.

But the comparative rate of growth of the two sections of the population for the decade 1891-1901 is a
fresh surprise. In Manitoba the tendency is least advanced; the rural gain was 65 per cent., while the urban
was 71; in British Columbia it is much more marked,
rural gain being 37 per cent. and urban 142; while in
Quebec the rural gain was 0.39 per cent. and the urban
31. In Prince Edward Island a rural loss of 5.8 per
cent. stands beside an urban gain of 4.7; in New Brunswick, a loss of 6.7 beside a gain of 36.7; in Nova Scotia,
a loss of 11 per cent. beside a gain of 40; and in Ontario,
a rural loss of 3.73 beside an urban gain of 12.49; while
through all Canada a rural increase of 53,375 is offset
by an urban increase of 484,701, or a gain of 1.01 per
cent. in rural by a gain of 31.53 in urban population.
But even yet we are scarcely prepared to find that in
New Brunswick there was an actual decline in rural

population in 84 per cent. of the census districts; in
Nova Scotia of 95 per cent.; in Ontario, exclusive of
the immigration areas in newly opened territory in
Algoma, Muskoka and Nipissing, of 98 per cent., and
in Prince Edward Island of 100 per cent. Let us present a few outstanding examples of retrogression covering longer periods, such as Durham East, with a total
population, including the town of Port Hope, of 19,064
in 1871, of 18,710 in 1881, of 17,053 in 1891, of
14,464 in 1901, and of 14,301 in 1911; Durham West,
including such a town as Bowmanville, with a total
population for those decades respectively of 18,316,
17,555, 15,374, 13,106, and 12,112; of Frontenac, as
formerly constituted—in all these comparative state-
ments we are careful to include strictly the same territory—with 16,310, 14,993, 13,445, 12,008, and 11,044;
or Lanark North, though such a town as Almonte is
included, with 19,899, 19,855, 19,260, 18,180, and
15,456; or Lennox, 16,396, 16,314, 14,900, 13,421, and
12,023; Northumberland West, 17,328, 16,948, 14,947,
13,055, and 12,965; or finally, Perth South, with
22,715, 21,608, 19,400, 17,861, and 16,038. Did considerations of space not forbid we should wish to add
detailed examples of retrogression in the case of townships covering the same period, inasmuch as the percentage of loss would be much more striking; for example, the township of Chinguacousy in the county of
Peel has this record—we go back ten years further—
in 1861, 6,897; 1871, 6,129; 1881, 5,467; 1891, 4,794;
1901, 4,177; and 1911, 3,913; a loss of 46 per cent. in
fifty years. An impressive array of similar histories
might be given. We close with one additional presentation of these momentous facts. The rural population

of Ontario in 1871 was 1,306,405. It is now 1,194,785.
There has been a loss in forty years of 111,620. Her
urban population was then 313,446. It is now
1,328,489. There has been a gain of 1,015,043. In all
eastern Canada there was in 1871 a rural population of
2,898,486. There is now 2,864,713, a loss in 40 years
of 23,773. There was then in all eastern Canada an
urban population of 680,296. There is now 2,599,228.
There has been an urban growth in forty years of
1,918,932.

In Quebec the problem assumes a special form. All of
the forces at work elsewhere are at work there also, with
an added one—racial dispossession. Originally all
of that great triangle of territory between the
United States border and the St. Lawrence River as
far down as Quebec was, save for a fringe of counties
along the St. Lawrence and of parishes along the
Richelieu, settled by English-speaking people. To-day,
through the action of a movement displacing and replacing one people by another, this great region, containing
fifteen counties—one of the finest in all Canada—is
overwhelmingly French-speaking.

This is not the first time in history that civilization
has been confronted with a problem arising out of the
displacement of one people by another. In ancient
Britain it arose at the close of the first half of the fifth
century. For a century and a half the problem pressed.
Then it passed. It was not solved. It ceased. A race
was extinguished. When Hengist landed on Thanet
in 449 Roman culture stretched across Britain and
reached the farthest shores of Ireland. It was the vigorous civilization which later made Ireland the chosen
home of letters and arts. When Llywarch sang the

death-song of Cyndyllan he sang the dirge of a passing people.

In one respect—that of race—we wish to draw a parallel between this movement and that now going on in Canada. The Saxon conquest was sheer dispossession. The historian Green tells us that " not a Briton remained as subject or slave on English ground." There was no massacre. But " field by field, forest by forest, the land was won. As each bit of ground was torn away by the stranger, the Briton sullenly withdrew, only to turn and fight doggedly for the next." Elsewhere, in Spain and Gaul, though these lands were also conquered by Germanic peoples, there was no dispossession. Religion, social life, administrative order, remained Roman. But in Britain the laws, the manners and the faith which the Roman people had left behind vanished before the Saxon. Just such a race movement is going on in Canada in our time. Robert Sellar, in his valuable monograph, " The Tragedy of Quebec," tells us that when he first went to Huntingdon, the county, save for one municipality, was as solidly English-speaking in population as any county in Ontario, but that he has witnessed the decline of the original people to the point of being in a minority. The same change, only in a more marked degree, has taken place in all the counties east of the Richelieu. Missisquoi, founded by U. E. Loyalists, has ceased to be English-speaking. Drummond, Wolfe, Shefford, may be said to be French-speaking. The transformation has been going on with startling rapidity during the past fifteen years. In 1891 there were eleven English-speaking counties in the Province of Quebec. Now English-speaking people are in a minority in every one. The writer is on familiar ground

3

in discussing this problem. In his boyhood there were only two French-speaking families in the village of Ormstown. A few years ago he attended a political meeting there. Chairman and speakers were French. A fragment of the time was given to an address in English.

It is unfortunate that this matter has to be referred to in terms of race, inasmuch as it is not racial in essential character. There is absolutely no racial barrier to prevent our French and English-speaking peoples commingling. In the writer's mind one French-Canadian, who was throughout his boyhood and youth employed on his father's farm, stands as a type of a splendid race. He had the physical hardihood that enabled him to handle a logging-chain bare-handed in the woods in winter, the mechanical aptitude which made all his work artistic in finish, the *bonhomie* of spirit which kept him ever genial and sprightly, and the faithfulness of character which made every task, however remote from oversight, not eye-service, but good-will. The respect and the affection with which the French-Canadian is regarded by the British-Canadian where he is intimately known is returned with reciprocal affection and respect. Witness Sir Wilfrid Laurier's tribute to Mr. Murray, his host in school days while he gained his rare mastery of the English tongue. Yet we have a race-movement in Canada planned with consummate skill and carried out with tenacity of purpose, affecting the population of wide extents of territory.

The problem given us by this race-movement is not simply one of ministering to the weakened remnant; not, for example, how to care for the 12,000 children of scattered English-speaking parents attending the French schools. It is rather how to stem the movement itself and hold our two races as one associated people. Quebec, apart from any question of population, holds the future of the Dominion in her hands. By the incorporation of Ungava she is rendered permanently our premier Province in extent. She is our greatest in resources. That province is the coming industrial centre of this continent. Of Canada's water-power, estimated at twenty-six million horse-power, Quebec is reported to possess seventeen million.* A mutual understanding and collaboration is needed for the efficient development of material resources of such magnitude, as well as for the political and social well-being of our common country.

Shall we not all be ONE race, shaping and wielding the nation?
 Is not our country too broad for the schisms which shake petty lands?
Yea, we shall join in our might, and keep sacred our firm federation,
 Shoulder to shoulder arrayed, hearts open to hearts, hands to hands! †

Nor is the problem confined to Quebec. In old Glengarry, known to fame, the majority of the population is French-speaking. Father Le Bel, speaking at the Parle Français Congress in Quebec in June last, is reported in the press as having stated that there are now 250,000 French-speaking people in Ontario, and that there are

* Mr. R. E. Young, Superintendent of Dominion Railway Lands, in testimony before the Forests, Waterways and Waterpowers Commission. Press report.
† Barry Stratton, " 85."

over 50,000 children taught in French in the bilingual
and the purely French schools of the Province.   Mr.
Frank Yeigh, the well-known publicist, informs us in
" Facts about Canada " that they have the preponderant
vote in fifteen counties; Father Le Bel claims that in
twenty-two their vote is the decisive factor.   Mr Yeigh
estimates that by the end of this century they will number six millions in Ontario.   Here in these beautiful
Muskoka groves—if the present tendencies remain un-
checked—before two generations shall have passed,
French, save on the lips of tourists, will be the only
language heard.   In New Brunswick the French population now numbers 90,000, or more than one-fourth of
the population.   In Prince Edward Island, while the
total population decreased by nine and a half thousand,
the French people increased by over four thousand.
This problem, then, is not a Quebec problem, but Canadian.   It is one of the greatest, if not the greatest, before any English-speaking nation to-day.

The first and fundamental dimension of the problem
is physical—the numerical diminution of the population.   But the rural loss is not only quantitative; it is
qualitative as well.   The second dimension is social,
and is measured by the strain on all social institutions
and relations.   Farm homes in Canada are farther apart
than anywhere else in the world.   Leaving out of consideration such districts as Algoma West, with 1.29 to the
square mile, and Algoma East, with 0.91, we have in
Ontario counties such as Lennox and Addington, 14.4;
South Renfrew, 14.1; North Lanark, 13.9; Frontenac,
13.1; Peterborough, 13.2; Victoria, 9.22.   In all these
cases the towns are included.   The rural population of
the United States is 15 to the square mile, and even

IN PRINCE EDWARD ISLAND, A TOWNSHIP LOSING 37 PER CENT. IN A DECADE.

The Garden of the Gulf, growing depleted.

Russia, whose people, moreover, live in hamlets rather than on farmsteads, has 16. Yet in Nova Scotia, Annapolis, including the towns has only 14.04; Shelburne and Queen's, 11.97; and Guysborough, 10.29; and New Brunswick as a Province, including her cities, has but 12.61 to the square mile.

How serious, therefore, is our situation when we find that under the first count in the social strain—the abandoned home—in Ontario, Lennox and Addington have 366 fewer dwelling houses than ten years ago, a loss of 6.9 per cent.; East Huron 310 less, a loss of 7.5 per cent.; North Lanark had 265 of its dwellings, or 7.7 per cent., go out of use in the decade; and Lambton East 491, or 8.3 per cent.; while in Grenville 352, or 9.17 per cent. became unoccupied—the largest loss, for a county, in the Province. But here again the county does not present the real facts; in towns the dwellings are increasing in number. The townships form the real test. Here are some of the outstanding instances. The historic township of East Zorra in Oxford County closed 13.6 per cent. of its homes; in Hastings, Madoc lost 13.7; Ashfield, in Huron, allowed 15 per cent. to fall into desuetude; in Grey, Egremont has 15.1 abandoned homes, and Glenelg, 16.2; Edwardsburg has 17 per cent.; Darling, in Lanark, 17.3; Cavan, in Durham, 18.8; Glenelg, also in Grey, 19.8 per cent. Were there space we might specify as well Arran, Culross, Huron, Wawanosh, Camden, Rochester, Greenock, Augusta, Brant, Tuscarora, Kinloss, Bruce, Haldimand, and Abinger, with empty farmhouses ranging from 10 to 20 per cent. But all of these are quite outclassed by Barrie, in Frontenac, with 25.4 of its dwellings abandoned in the decade; Morris, in Huron, with 25.5;

Keppel, in Grey, 27.17, and Sarawak, in Grey, 45.8 per cent. The loss is as widespread in the Maritime Provinces as in Ontario. In New Brunswick, Hampton lost 36 per cent. of its homes, Hillsborough 39, Sussex 46, St. Francis 49, and Madawaska 58 per cent. Not poetic sentiment only but stern fact in fancy drest is given us in the lines:

> Memory gleams like a gem at night
>   Through the gloom of to-day to me,
> Bringing dreams of a childhood bright
>   At Chateauguay.

> Stands a house by the river side,
>   Weeds upspring where the hearth should be,
> Only its tottering walls abide,
>   At Chateauguay.*

But the abandoned dwelling is a lesser social evil than the weakened household. While engaged in pastoral visiting lately, a parishioner spoke to me of the number of houses in his neighborhood from which a multitude once went with him to the house of God to keep holyday. But the pathos of the situation was seen in this, that he himself was living in his well-found house alone. From Edwardsburg we lost in the decade one-eleventh of our families, but one-fifth of our population. The families which remain are depleted households in the midst of a depleted countryside. From the families which are still with us in Grenville there have gone away 1,303 persons. This does not mean that simply the redundant members of the household leave. It means that in many cases parents are left to carry on the farm alone. Let

* Arthur Weir, "Fleur de Lys."

Grenville stand as our single and sufficient illustration.
In 1901 the average number of persons per family in
city and country throughout Canada was 5.16. In
Grenville it was then 4.42. By 1911 the average for
Canada in city and country had fallen to 4.84. But in
Grenville it had fallen to 4.07. Family life that averages only four persons to a household throughout a community of over seventeen thousand persons can suffer
little further diminution and continue.

The third line of social strain is seen in the relative
numbers of the sexes in rural Canada. One of the most
startling surprises given by the recent census was found
in the lessened proportion of women in our country
homes. The girls are even more dissatisfied with farm
life than are the boys, and are leaving in larger numbers.

The general rule of population the world over is that
females outnumber males. The usual proportion is
about 105 to 100 at birth, and about 107 to 100 in adult
life. This rule holds good of our urban population. In
only 45 out of the 250 cities, towns and villages of older
Ontario do males exceed females. But in our rural
population this universal rule of human life is reversed,
and the reversal is so general as to be astounding. In
only 40 of the 920 townships and other rural divisions—
exclusive of Indian reserves—enumerated by the census
in all Ontario do females outnumber males.

Let us take the county of Middlesex as an illustration.
In the North Riding there are six townships. In every
case males exceed females, and the total excess is 473.
The riding contains also one town, Parkhill, and two
villages, Ailsa Craig and Lucan. In all, women surpass
men in number, the whole surplus being 188. East

Middlesex is purely rural, consisting of the four fine townships of London, Dorchester, Nissouri, and Westminster. In each the male population predominates, the aggregate predominance being 518. The west riding embraces five townships; in every one more men than women are found, the plurality throughout the five being 469. In its town and villages, Strathroy, Glencoe, Newbury and Wardsville, men are everywhere in a minority, its total being 355. There is one city within the bounds of the county, London, with an excess of females over males of 2,498. In the townships of Middlesex there are 107 men to 100 women. In the city, towns and villages of Middlesex there are 112 women to 100 men. There is only one county in Ontario, this one of Grenville, in which females exceed males in the purely rural population.

The excess of females over males in the urban population of Ontario is 10,865. The excess of males over females in the rural population of Ontario is 85,940. In the cities, towns and villages, taken by themselves, there are 102 women to 100 men. In town and country taken together there are 106 men to 100 women. In the country alone there are 116 men to 100 women.

This anomaly holds true, not of Ontario only, but of all rural Canada. In New Brunswick males outnumber females in every census district except the city of St. John. There women outrank men by 2,013. In the rest of the Province men outrank women by 7,845. In Nova Scotia in every district outside of Halifax save two there is an excess of females. The overplus for the province is 9,700.

Have all of our women the vagrant heart? We know

that they have not. Then why so many fleeing from the country ?

Ah, to be a woman! to be left to pique and pine,
When the winds are out and calling to this vagrant heart of
    mine,
Whisht! it whistles at the windows, and how can I be still?
There! the last leaves of the beech-tree go dancing down the
    hill.
All the boats at anchor they are plunging to be free—
Oh! to be a sailor, and away across the sea!
O bird that fights the heavens, and is blown beyond the shore,
Would you leave your flight and danger for a cage, to fight
    no more?
No more the cold of winter, or the hunger of the snow,
Nor the winds that blow you backward from the path you
    wish to go?
Would you leave your world of passion for a home that knows
    no riot?
Would I change my vagrant longings for a heart more full of
    quiet?
No—for all its dangers, there is joy in danger, too;
On, bird, and fight your tempests, and this nomad heart with
    you!*

But where there is not the vagrant spirit, what impels our girls to leave ?

A fourth form of social strain ought perhaps to be discussed. It is said that leaders are leaving the country. Those who are drawn away include many of the ablest and most progressive. There are, however, higher qualities than ability and energy. I have known of more than one case where young men, and of still more cases where young women, remained on the farm

* Dora Sigerson Shorter, " A Vagrant Heart."

through a sense of duty to others. Efficient help is
given in the solution of more than one direct problem
by actions such as this. Duty is the source of energy.

The drain meanwhile is real. Our question is only
as to the validity of the principle. I visited recently a
farm home in the county of Dundas. My host, after
having—according to the farmer's manner—shown me
something of his barns, brought me to his office. It was
furnished with roll-top desk, desk telephone, safe, and
reference library. Everything about home and farm
was in keeping therewith. Yet the household consisted
of husband and wife, hired woman and hired man. But
there were three sons and two daughters in the city. The
eldest son is a graduate—with honors in mathematics—
of Toronto University, and has passed the examinations
of the Institute of Actuaries of Great Britain. The
other sons are graduates in Medicine and in Science of
McGill University. The eldest daughter is a graduate
of the Conservatory of Music at Toronto. The children
will not consent to the sale of the farm. It is still the
home of their pride, the scene of their happy vacations
and reunions. Such cases are not uncommon. But does
it follow that the country must deteriorate? Can we
afford to obey the mandate:

> Go, bind your sons to exile,
> Send forth the best ye breed.

That depends solely on the spirit of those who remain.
If part go that they may achieve something worth while,
their very going proves a spur to all who take pride in
their success. For centuries the achievements of Scotland's sons abroad were the very pulse of life to her sons
at home. But when hopelessness or dissatisfaction is

the cause of the exodus, blight comes, not because of the
exodus, but of abiding conditions. The country can
obey the maxim, " Send forth the best ye breed," provided that she " take up the White Man's burden ";
can " bind her sons to exile " if it be " to serve another's
need." That call " comes now, to search your manhood," not to impair it. What is needed is intense life
—not labor, but life—upon the farm itself, so that the
country shall not become the byway. The highway
must lie free for all through city and country alike.

> This is the law of the highways,
>   This is their gospel made plain,
> Let the laggards keep to the byways,
>   And the weak and the halt remain,
> Where the hurrying tides shall heed not,
>   And the eyes of the world shall not see,
> The weaklings of life that we need not,
>   In these paths where the strong must go free.
>
> Age decrepit, and youth
>   Streaked with age ere its prime,
> The crafty side-trackers of truth,
>   The thriftless consumers of time,
> Mere shadow-shapes of man,
>   And woman worn to a shade,
> These do the highways ban,
>   And with iron brows upbraid.
>
> This is the law of the highways,
>   This is their gospel writ wide,
> Let the souls that are formed for the byways
>   Keep clear of our strenuous tide,
> For patience we have not, nor space,
>   For the weak, or the halt, or the blind,
> For the aged that cannot keep pace,
>   Nor the eyes that are looking behind.*

* J. C. M. Duncan, in *The Witness*, Montreal.

This is the law of the country and has been. Not hers " the thriftless consumers of time." The virile country not only can " bind her sons to exile to serve another's need "; she " dare not stoop to less." And if for the hour despondent, she is true at the heart to her past.

The third count in our problem amounts to the question: Is there a moral strain being placed upon rural life by our present situation? In this field it is more difficult to glean representative facts and present them fairly. No statistics are available on this aspect of the problem. Dr. W. L. Anderson, in his able volume dealing with our problem, writes: " Our argument rests upon the favorable showing of the country as a whole compared with the city as a whole. As tested by the symptoms of degeneracy, the country is in as healthful a state as the city; where the advantages and wholesome influences of civilization are massed; where education is at its best; where eloquence finds its opportunity and art gathers its treasures; where wealth gathers all resources and taste has every gratification; where churches are powerful and every social institution co-operates in the exaltation of human life. That the country is not distanced by the city in social and moral development almost exceeds belief; or, to use the terms in which we began, the line of averages is at a surprising height in the country."* The question is, however, not one of comparative values in city and country, but of what tendencies are at work in the country.

Country life of late has made one marked advance. It has socialized, and to a large extent solved, the drink

* W. L. Anderson, " The Country Town," p. 111.

problem. It has taken hold of this evil as a community question and has therefore crowned its efforts with success. It has not only socialized the reform, but to some degree standardized it as well. The country newspaper has to a very large extent barred out the liquor advertisement. And to this standard the urban press must come.

I might add that the country has made marked advance in regard to general practice concerning the use of tobacco. Last autumn seventeen farmers, chiefly young men, gathered at the home of one of my church managers on silo-filling day. Of the seventeen not one used tobacco in any form.

Business integrity, in so far as tested by the older ethical standards, is high in the country. But it is not yet so in regard to the newer ethical imperatives. A daughter of the manse and a daughter of the farm were discussing some finer branch of cooking. " But we use cream, not milk," said the daughter of the farm. " Oh," was the response, " do you keep the milk of a cow at home just for that ?" " Pshaw, no," came the answer, " we take a dipper or two from the factory can." This is suggestive of much that is lacking bearing upon the ethics of co-operation in the country.

In other fields having to do with graver moral evils I offer no attempt at generalization. But let me give single instances of actualities in several moral realms. Near a certain hamlet which shall be nameless a farmer sent his wife into the field to drive the team with the harrows. When, wearied, she sat down to rest, he rent a splinter from a fence rail and beat her. By night men forced his door, dragged him from hiding, rode him upon a fence rail, and informed him that if he beat his wife again treatment more drastic would be meted out to him. Here two grave crimes meet: wife-beating and lynch-law. What is the bearing upon our problem? A farmer of Canadian stock had sold and left that farm; he had been replaced by an immigrant of a stock morally lower than our Canadian farmers, among whom wife-beating is unknown.

In the home of another young man in that hamlet two women were frequently left alone—his wife and another. The public noticed with disapproval the occasional coming of some men of leisure from a neighboring city, the nation's capital. One night, while one of these was present, the men of the place turned out and gave the house a "charivari," staining its walls with broken eggs, and withdrew. Soon afterwards the premises were sold, and the household went away into oblivion. Again the bearing upon our problem is this: The young husband, finding little occupation at his trade in the neighborhood, sought employment away from home in the town.

Again, the township of Edwardsburg has, like all other Ontario townships, been almost unstained by the crime of murder. Yet we had one sad case in recent years. A man who had purchased a farm raised his hand against the man from whom he had bought it. The verdict of the jury, with the full assent of the Attorney-General, was "Insanity"; and, what is more, the verdict of our people, a community of whom the great majority would never condone crime even to save one of their number from death, unanimously acquiesced in the verdict. But who was he who was thus acquitted of responsibility for his deed? The trend citywards had called away a son from that home to the city, for whose life he was unfitted; and the father, to bring him back from the city, made over to him the homestead, and purchasing elsewhere for himself that he might begin anew, had broken down under the strain.

For an illustration from another field of moral evil we shall go beyond our own borders. Mr. P. V. Collins, editor of the *Northwestern Agriculturalist,* of Minneapolis, advertised for a stenographer of the highest ability. From among the applications received he selected one from a young woman apparently of such qualifications as he desired. But when she came to his office he discovered that she had only a public school education and a rudimentary knowledge of shorthand. When asked why she had copied out the application she replied, " I did not write that; the principal of the academy which gave me my diploma sent it." Investigation brought out the facts that there was a bogus college selling diplomas throughout the country to anyone who had been for a term at a business school; and then sending country girls to positions which they could not possibly fill, notifying those in charge of the traffic in immorality of the stranding of the girls in the city. This particular one met with a philanthropist and friend, but there are other cases. The longing to escape from country to town is being taken advantage of by designing men to lure girls to their ruin.

But the chief factor in the moral strain is not found in the direct evil results or the moral pitfalls incident to the situation, but in the fact that moral enthusiasms are lacking in the country owing to the present trend. No high incentive takes men away; no lofty passion abides with those who remain. Where people are discontent with their lot and seek to escape it, with no fine aspiration leading them to any other walk in life, there is an absence of the moral incentives which made rural morality so splendid a thing in the past.

There is the best of testimony to the existence of the moral strain. Professor Giddings writes: " Degeneration manifests itself in the protean forms of suicide, insanity, crime and vice which abound in the highest civilization where the tension of life is extreme, and in those places from which civilization has ebbed away, leaving a discouraged remnant to struggle against deteriorating conditions. . . . Like insanity, crime occurs most frequently in densely populated towns on the one hand, and on the other in partly deserted rural districts."* Dr. H. B. MacCauley, Secretary of the Eastern Division of the Federal Council of the Churches of Christ in America, says: " In my district of thirteen States I have an opportunity of seeing the condition of things in the country in a way that is very broad; and I am prepared to say that if there is a place anywhere that needs the remedy which Jesus Christ alone can give, that place is in the country."†

In the connection that obtains between the church and our problem there is a two-fold reference: the bearing of the situation upon the church, and the relation of the church to the problem.

The bearing of the situation upon the church is manifest. The church is sensitively sympathetic to every vital experience of the community. The immediate result of depopulation is the loss of numbers to the church. This has not as yet been proportionate to the decline in

* F. H. Giddings, "Principles of Sociology," p. 348.
† "The Rural Church and Community Betterment," p. 38.

population. The church is holding her own better than other institutions in the country. But a glance shows the inevitable trend. That trend is common to all denominations. Surveys of rural conditions made recently in the United States show conclusively that the increase or the decrease of the churches is a communal experience. Where one suffers all suffer with it. Investigation would doubtless show the same to be the case in Canada. But let us look at representative facts as found in the Presbyterian Church in Canada.

When we open the Blue-book the first congregation found on the official list in the Statistical Tables is Boularderie, in Sydney Presbytery. Let us look over its record for a decade. Its households numbered in 1902, 290; in 1903, 274; in 1904, 270; in 1905 the pastorate was vacant and no returns are given; in 1906, 250; 1907, 249; 1908, 246; 1909, 246; 1910, 231; 1911, 161. The severe loss in the last year is doubtless due in some way to the extension of the plant of the Steel and Coal Company at Sydney; the steady decline for the decade reflects general conditions. This congregation was taken simply because it stood first upon the list. Let us take a larger unit, a Presbytery, by selection as a representative one. Lanark and Renfrew may fairly be called such. It lies in a fertile and progressive district. It has an excellent record in church activities. Its congregations are strong, the self-supporting ones averaging 130 households to the pastoral charge. The average stipend or salary of its rural ministers is above $1,000. It appears to increase. It contained 3,362 households in 1901 and 3,763 in 1911, an increase of 401 for the decade. Let us see how this increase is accounted for. Six mission fields have been founded in new districts, with an aggregate of 188 families. The increase of the Presbytery as it existed in 1901 is but 213 households. There were at that time—including missions—33 charges. Of these two now number just what they did in 1901; 13 show an increase—of these two only are purely rural; 18 show a decrease. But the increase in the congregations in the towns of Arnprior, Renfrew and Smith's Falls is 284 families. There is therefore a loss throughout the rest of the Presbytery, including the towns of Almonte, Carleton Place, Pembroke and Perth, of 71 households; while the falling off in the 18 congregations actually losing amounts to 215. The facts underlying the total figures when analyzed in this Presbytery would be found typical elsewhere. But let us take a wider unit still. The three central Synods increased in each case steadily from 1901 to 1909 in the number of families. Then there comes an ominous change in all three cases. The Synod of Montreal and Ottawa had in 1909, 21,720 households. In 1910 it had 21,276, a decline of 444. Toronto and Kingston in the former year had 42,507, in the latter 42,176, a decrease of 331. Hamilton and London in 1909 numbered 28,243; in 1910, 28,037, a falling off of 206. The latter recovers in 1911 to 28,784; Montreal and Ottawa recovers to 21,637, but is still short of the mark of two years before; Toronto and Kingston had still further fallen to 40,986, an added loss of 1,521 households. We may perhaps realize the trend most vividly by noticing that six Presbyteries suffered loss in the total number of households in the decade, namely Kingston, Lindsay, Barrie, Saugeen, Stratford, and Bruce, with an aggregate decline of 963 families; while the Presbyteries of

PRESBYTERIAN CHURCH, SPENCERVILLE.
A village cathedral, built in better days.

Hamilton, Montreal, and Toronto, though each, while largely urban, includes a rural section, increased respectively by 1,780, 2,086, and 4,768 households. In each case the gain was considerably more than half of the total gain in the whole corresponding synod for the decade.

Rural churches are not and cannot be filled with worshippers as they once were. The Presbyterian Church in Spencerville, a village cathedral built in better days, never puts its spacious gallery to use. The most easterly church in the Presbytery of Glengarry, in Ontario, and the most westerly one in the Presbytery of Montreal, in Quebec. are examples of churches whose auditoriums have been cut down in size since they were first built. Churches here and there are closed. Within six miles of Spencerville are two churches whose congregations dwindled until they disappeared. No statistics are available upon this aspect of the problem in Canada. But in the United States, where the strain upon the churches has proved much more severe than in Canada, accurate surveys show the situation. The Ohio Rural Life Survey of 1912, for instance, reveals 800 abandoned churches in that State. In no county in the State are one-half of the congregations holding their own. In several counties not 10 per cent. are growing. In 10 counties, with a total of 394 congregations, not one-twentieth of the number had resident ministers. The ministers live in towns and go to the country to preach. Ninety-six townships in these ten counties, comprising nearly 4,000 square miles, are without a resident minister in the country districts.

Other bearings of the situation upon the church in addition to this fundamental one might be discussed;

we confine ourselves to the falling off in students for the
ministry. This is forcibly presented for one branch of
the church by Professor Kilpatrick in his Introduction
to Mr. Mott's volume, " The Future Leadership of the
Church." " The Blue-book for 1908 presents facts
worthy of careful consideration. In 1875 the church
possessed 139 students; in 1907 this number had risen
to 194, a gain of 55. In 1875 the church possessed 706
charges; in 1907 this number had risen to 1,984, a gain
of 1,278. If it required 139 students to supply the
needs of a church of 706 congregations, surely 194 are
far too few to supply the needs of a church of 1,984 congregations. Again, compare 1907 with 1902. In 1902
the church possessed 230 students and 997 congregations. In 1907 the number of congregations had increased by 987, while the number of students had decreased by 36." The cause of this decline is found in
the rural situation. Over 90 per cent. of our students
have been drawn from the country. The increasing discontent and unrest, the lessening of optimism and altruism, have affected adversely the country's richest product, the heralds of the Cross.

Of more importance is the church's relation to the
problem. The church is a means, not an end. The
question is not one of maintaining her numbers and
recruiting her ranks. It is one of the efficacy of her
service to the country in its need. There was a time
when the chancelleries of Europe were hard pressed to
provide revenue for their governments. Then the
science of political economy had its birth. The chancelleries found that the best way to secure revenue was
by making their people prosperous. There was a period
when for ages the Christian Church thought the end of

her existence was the perfection of her own organism, and the cathedrals of Europe form the magnificent monument of the ideal and of its failure. The purpose of our enquiry is not in the slightest degree, How can the Church save herself amid the country's peril? It is, How can she make rural life a happier and nobler life, how she can meet the unmet needs of Canada, until

From Nova Scotia's misty coast to far Columbia's shore
She wakes—a band of scattered homes and wilderness no more,
But a strong nation, with her life full-beating in her breast,
A noble future in her eyes—the Britain of the West.

Hers be the noble task to fill the yet untrodden plains
With fruitful, many-sided life that courses through her veins;
The earnest quest of noble ends,—the generous heart of youth,—
The stamp of true nobility, high honor, stainless truth;

The love of country soaring far above dull party strife,
The love of learning, art, and song—the crowning grace of life;
The love of science searching far through nature's hidden ways;

The love and fear of nature's God—a nation's highest praise;
The English honor, nerve, and pluck,—the Scotsman's love of right,—
The grace and courtesy of France,—the Irish fancy bright,—
The Saxon's faithful love of home and home's affections blest;
And, chief of all, our holy faith—of all our treasures best!*

* Agnes Maule Machar, " Dominion Day."

ECONOMIC CAUSES OF DEPLETION

rich farm lands of the Chateauguay Valley in Quebec, goes vividly back to the year 1869. A shy and visionary boy, I watched the tradesmen at their work while other schoolboys strove upon the playground. In that year the ashery, unused for years, was dismantled—the scene of an earlier, already vanished industry. In the sawmill work was being urged with pressing haste. Night shifts were often employed. At the grist mill farmers contested for precedence as they brought great loads of fine-hulled white oats to be kiln-dried and ground into round Scotch oatmeal, with sleighloads of which they then drove to distant Montreal to market. This mill was a few years later enlarged to meet the increasing local demand for its output of flour. Near the centre of the village stood the tannery, one of our largest buildings. All manipulations, from flesher to currier, were by hand; and from the bark-mill in the broad shed to the harness-shop in the upper storey the establishment was a scene of busy industry. The portly tanner who then initiated his boy follower into the mysteries of bark-pit and ooze I learned in later years to know as an excellent Shakespearean scholar. Nearby was the principal cabinet-maker's shop. A sweep horsepower in the basement drove the turning-lathe at which bed-posts and spindles were fashioned. At the side benches apprentice and journeymen worked, while at the front bench the proprietor—a village philanthropist and the patriarch of the temperance forces of the Province—wrought in walnut or bird's-eye maple the bridal suites of furniture for the community. The six wood-working shops of the village were each distinctive in character. At the oldest of the house-carpenter shops the coffins for the dead of the countryside were also made, each as sad occasion called. And into the making of each went a loving sympathy unknown in an age of machine-made products. As if it were yesterday there comes back the sense of the mystery of death and of fellow-feeling with bereavement which workman and little boy by his side, permitted to hold and pass the silvered nails, alike felt as the work went on in reverent silence. Another of the local carpenters was then building the spacious village church, portrayed at page 195 of this volume, producing every panel and moulding on the spot and by hand, save as a treadmill horse-power, set up temporarily on the premises, lent its aid. From the homes of each of these builders a youth afterwards entered the ministry. Another of our carpenters specialized in the exact work of the millwright, and showed himself in various ways a self-taught mathematical genius. In my university days I discovered that he, who had never seen a copy of Euclid, had, Pascal-like, wrought out at his bench many of the problems of Euclid. At the wheelwright shops all vehicles for pleasure-driving as well as for farm use were built. I can recall seeing farmers drive in with loads of split hickory bolts for spokes and rock-elm blocks for hubs, though already the machine-made spoke and hub were competing for favor. The ironwork on these vehicles was no assemblage of machine-made parts, but the product of genuine craftsmanship, elaborate and ornate. All the smiths of the neighborhood were master craftsmen. One, at Dewittville near by, specialized in forging steel, and for this service burned his own charcoal pits. As a lad of seven or eight I took delight in watching the neat conical piles of wood carefully laid, and seeing the strange gases ooze through the covering of clay, while creosote condensed and dripped from the inserted gun-barrel. How different the amount of labor bestowed on such products then and now! As we detrained at Longford to come over here to Geneva Park a day or two ago we passed one of the Canada Chemical Company's extensive plants, where by the carload wood is run, car and all, into the retort, and the car comes out at length with a load of charcoal upon it ready for shipment. Now, too, the distillates, formerly wasted, pay for both material and process, and the once costly charcoal is a clear-gain by-product.

In the open country on the other side of the village by the Chateauguay another smith—master alike of his trade and the situation—forged the long iron-frame plow, so heavy to turn at the furrow's end, but so light of draft upon the team because of true lines of design and fine workmanship. With that same long plow the plowmen of the days of my boyhood turned furrows so true in line and so clean in comb that a rifle bullet might be fired from end to end of the field on those level meadows without once rising above the crest of the furrow, yet without staining itself with touch of the clay. Presently there came to the village the machine-shop also, for local service, and for well-nigh a generation the threshing-machines for the locality were of home manufacture. Space forbids my describing other busy shops—those of the tailors, the shoemakers, the saddlers, and many another. In that small village of eight hundred people there were then over thirty-five such shop industries.

CHURCH AT SHANLY, ONTARIO.

An abandoned church, Grenville County.

Tradesmen such as these have as a class almost disappeared from our present-day industrial world. Their going deprives the countryside of a variety of openings in life for persons of different tastes, and confines the choice of occupations to one, that of agriculture. It has removed varied types of life from the community, reducing social groups to the monotony of a single class. It has withdrawn an intelligent, capable, prosperous and contented population from the country.

This loss is reflected in our literature:

This river of azure with many a weed in
  Its pools is as fair as those famous of old;
Its wash is the same as made blossoms in Eden,
  And still it remembers their crimson and gold;
As lovely this valley with forests around it,
  As vivid the evergreens shading the hill;
But manhood has gone from the cottage that crowned it,
  And alders are growing at Atkinson's Mill.

The stream is the same with its tinting of azure,
  Yet the old bridge is moved from its mooring of stone.
Departed are those who once made it a pleasure
  To sail here, or skate when the summer had flown.
This pathway through cedar is trampled no longer
  By feet that went daily to school 'gainst their will;
The fragrance of hope in the springtime was stronger
  And sweeter than summer by Atkinson's Mill.*

One of the chief steps in this process proved a serious blow to the prosperity of the Maritime Provinces—the cessation of the ship-building industry when the sailing vessel with wooden hull was replaced by the steel-built steamer. Before that time Canada had become fifth in rank among the mercantile maritime nations, Britain,

* Andrew Ramsay.

apart from Canada, ranking first. Our poets then sang
with pride:

> I see to every wind unfurled
> The flag that bears the maple-wreath;
> Thy swift keels furrow round the world,
> Its blood-red folds beneath;
> Thy swift keels cleave the farthest seas,
> Thy white sails swell with alien gales. . . . .*

and the building of these vessels gave our sea-board
cities economic and social wealth.

The cause of this loss lies in the genius of the modern
industrial world. The processes which have wrought
out this modern system destroyed an industrial order
which had been in building since the destruction of the
ancient Roman civilization. The characteristic mark
of this vanished order was household industry engaged
in local production for local use. The modern industrial world brought in the factory system and world-
wide transportation, each of which owes its rise to the
invention of machinery and the discovery of power, and
by means of these has developed its characteristic and
epitome, the modern city.

The year 1769, an even century before the date of our
description of village crafts, marks an epoch in the
world's history. In that year Arkwright patented his
spinning frame and set up his first mill equipped therewith, driven as yet by horse-power, but marking the beginning of the factory system. In that year Watt
patented his steam engine, which alone could have rendered the factory system effective. In the same decade,
another genius, James Brindley, gave to the world the

* Charles G. D. Roberts, " In Divers Tones."

modern canal system. The means of communication thus begun, augmented by the advent of the steamboat in 1807, and the railroad in 1830, rendered possible the massing of factories in great cities. New York ranked ninth of the cities of the United States in 1820, with but 9,000 people to Albany's 96,000, and was being still further outclassed. Her true growth began with the opening of the Erie Canal in 1825, but her rapid expansion about 1839 with the advent of the modern steamship. The Bessemer process, 1856, giving the steel rail instead of the iron one, cut the cost of railway haulage in half. Power transmission in 1891 rendered possible a still greater concentration by placing factories, not at the place of the source of power, but at the foci of transport and centres of trade. The average cost of transport in 1800 was ten dollars per ton per hundred miles. As I write a carload of mill-feed has just come into Spencerville from Brandon. The cost of transport is four dollars per ton for one thousand five hundred miles. For wheat and flour the cost was then prohibitive at two hundred miles distance. Now they can be profitably carried by rail and sea the semi-circumference of the earth.

Another concurrent change has had an equally great effect in industrial organization. The incorporated company was called into being by the need for larger aggregations of capital; the corporate trust—of which the Standard Oil Trust, originating in 1881, was the prototype—was designed to eliminate the wastes of competition, but has been used to limit production, control prices, and monopolize markets. Thus has arisen an industrial economy which syndicates each form of production over the area of a continent and seeks to incorporate the world.

The direct result of these changes has been that articles in all lines of production are made more cheaply in large factories with power machines than in the small shops by hand labor. The demand for the latter, except in some lines of artistic production, has ceased. The master workman dismissed his journeyman and apprentices, and eventually betook himself with his household to the city, to become factory operatives.

The final outcome has been an almost inconceivably great increase in material production, together with a general advance in conditions of living, but with lamentable failure to reap the full advantage in human welfare of the new conditions. The strain of toil has been lightened, hours of labor have been shortened, scarcity of the necessities of life has largely ceased; men are housed and clad and fed with such comfort and plenty as our forefathers never knew. But at every step of the process the persons displaced have suffered hardship. Wealth has increased enormously, but an undue share of the reward has gone into the hands of the few. New realms are made subject to our command, but in the process the human element has been too much disregarded. A system which gives us the automobile, but which also gives us the rubber atrocities in Congo and Peru for the sake of our automobile tires—and wrongs more widespread if not so deadly here at home—demands control in some way by the Spirit of God through Jesus Christ.

Yet the modern industrial system is not the cause, but merely the occasion of such failure. It has furnished some with a greater engine of oppression than any had ever before possessed, only because it has afforded to all a greater means of service than any ever before known.   In the material framework of the industrial world we have the structural lines supplied us upon which the finest spiritual development man has as yet conceived of shall presently take place.   " One music, as before, but vaster," shall yet arise from the modern world.   The new is better than the old.

Moreover, the change is not only for the better, it was also imperative.   Malthus was entirely in the right in asserting, from his standpoint amidst the economic conditions of his time, that population was rapidly pressing upon the limits of the means of subsistence. Though the greater portion of the race was then engaged in agriculture, food production was insufficient for increase of population, whereas now greater abundance for all is furnished by the moiety of the population which still remains upon the land, and every prospect promises greater abundance for yet larger population for indefinite periods in the future.

The opening up of new lands under the old economic conditions would not have bettered matters, inasmuch as agricultural regions such as Saskatchewan now is could not have become the base of support for more densely populated distant regions apart from modern means of transportation ; nor, indeed, could agricultural regions such as these have come into being, for their needed manufactured products could not have been transported to them.   All expansion must have been expansion of the limits of the community organized as it then was.

Not only so, but to Malthus's position we must add this—that population was pressing upon the limits of manufacture as well as of food supply, for man had

5

come to the limits of available power. It could, we are persuaded, be shown from the records of the time that the amount of power derived from the muscular energy of the horse and the ox had begun to diminish in proportionate quantity, and that derived from human muscles to increase. And for this underlying cause, that the power drawn from the labor of the horse and ox calls for a greater extent of land surface for food supply than does the same amount of power derived from the muscles of men. This is the explanation of the use of human labor in the heaviest tasks in China and Japan. The tourist is shocked as he listens to the forced respiration of the coolies while they haul carts laden with builders' materials up the Bluff at Yokohama; the philanthropist is stirred to indignation as he sees the Chinaman carry, poised on the head cradle, the heavy timbers of the Yunnan forests to their place of use on the Great Plain. I have seen teams of a thousand men, with intensest strain of the muscles, spurred on by the crack of the lash, haul the heavy hulls of junks up the inclined planes of mud which form the locks of the Grand Canal of China. Such human toil is due to the relative dearness of animal labor amidst a dense population as its sole cause. This, and not indifference to human suffering, this, and not lack of inventiveness, lays such loads upon the coolies of the Orient.

When the sedan chair was first used in England it was a common remark that men were made to do the work of beasts. The first letters patent for the keep of sedan chairs for hire in London were granted in order " to prevent the unnecessary use of coaches." As England increased further in population she must have

called other men from her looms to become porters of
the webs woven; she must have bidden her plowmen
become delvers of the soil.   In China the mattock
replaces the plow, and the roller is drawn, not by horses
or oxen, but by men.   To this pass Europe was coming,
was perilously near, when the power of steam came to
her rescue.   The world had come to a pass where advance in civilization or regression towards savagery
were the only paths possible.   There was no middle
way of stability.   The new order came to relieve alike
the weaver at the loom and the husbandman at the
plow.

The loss of village commerce is following that of the
village crafts.   A quarter of a century ago the village
storekeeper was a prosperous man.   He was not uncom-
monly the wealthiest man in the community.   His
place of business served, in a way, as a social centre.
His family, and he himself, were helpers and leaders
in every social enterprise, including the church.   Then
in 1876 John Wanamaker organized the Departmental
Store and the Mail Order System.   He had earlier
become a disciple of Ruskin in holding that chaffering
had no legitimate place in trade, and that an absolutely
one-price system must prevail.   Cheap and rapid tran-
sit made the mail-order system possible.   The one-price
system and exact description in advertising, together
with large turnover and direct service, made it efficient.
Retail trading has in consequence been revolutionized.
Wholesaling half a century ago was done over the
counter.   The country trader travelled to the city to
place his orders.   Then came the drummer, the modern
" commercial man."   As completely as wholesale trade
was thereby recast in new moulds, so fully is retailing

now being made over. We are in the last hours of the older day. Here, again, as in the case of the village crafts, the outcome has been an ultimate economic benefit, but an immediate social loss. Severe distress is felt by the class displaced. And the community loses one more of its progressive elements.

But the decrease in rural population is chiefly due to the removal from the country community of farmers' households. What is the explanation of their removal?

One factor in Eastern Canada was the opening up to settlement of the rich wheat lands of Manitoba by the building of the Canadian Pacific Railroad in 1885. The beginning of marked depletion of population in Ontario occurs in the following year, 1886. But another and more universal factor had been already at work for a generation, and was, just at that juncture, attaining full force. For the art of farming also was revolutionized by the introduction of machinery and of power. True, it was as early as 1834 that McCormick invented the reaper. But it was not until the Crystal Palace Exhibition in London in 1861—that revealer of so many tendencies—that the utility of the reaper was demonstrated. The year 1835 gave us the most primitive form of the thresher, but in 1864 the first steam thresher was used. In 1874 the binder came, but not until 1886 did its usefulness begin, when its fingers learned to knot twine instead of, as before, twisting wire. That year, in which the marked exodus of farmers from the Maritime Provinces and Ontario to Manitoba began, may fairly be said to begin a new period in agriculture. The year which brought in the twine-binder brought also the gang-plow and the use of steam power in plowing. In that year came also the somewhat rapid adoption of the silo. Just before that date the first cream separator to be used on this side of the Atlantic had been set up in the Province of Quebec. About the same period also began the widespread adoption of the modern barn, with its trolley unloader and its installation of a water system. The introduction of improved field machinery, the hay-loader, the potato-digger, the manure-spreader; the employment of the traction engine and the gasoline motor, has kept pace with the remodelling of the barn. The outcome of these changes is that one man, with modern equipment, can accomplish the results achieved by many in the days of hand labor. The Census Bureau of the United States, in a report dealing with the census of 1890, published a comparative table covering the nine principal farm products in 1850, and showing that whereas 570,000,000 days' labor—that of 1,900,000 persons for 300 days—were required to produce them, the same amount of the same staples in 1890 were accounted for by 400,000 persons or 120,000,000 days' labor, slightly over one-fifth requisite forty years before. The ratio of change during the ensuing twenty years has doubtless been accelerated rather than slackened. We would probably be not far wrong in supposing that the efficiency of labor, in the major operations at any rate, is not far from seven times what it was two generations ago.

But with the increasing use of machinery on the farm has come, with almost equal pace, an increasing demand for farm produce due to increase of city population and to the more lavish consumption accompanying increased wealth. The setting free from farm labor of a certain number follows the introduction of machinery as a matter of course. But why has there not also come fuller satisfaction with farm conditions? Why have we not, while the city grows, at least a stable farm population, with greatly enlarged production *per capita,* with increasing rural wealth, together with decreasing prices of farm produce, and with greatly enhanced leisure for better living on the farm?

The world's markets are not glutted with farm goods; the reverse is the case. Prices of farm products have not decreased, but have risen greatly. The steady, general upward trend of all prices is ultimately due to the cheapening of the standard of value—gold. But the proportionate increase in price of one great class of products above another is due to subsidiary causes. The incidence of higher prices upon those with fixed earnings is so severe as to constitute the greatest economic difficulty of our time.

Now, amidst all the increase in the cost of living, that due to enhanced prices of commodities from the farm stands easily first. In the year 1897, when the cost of living was at the lowest point reached for a generation, the index figure for all wholesale prices in Canada stood at 92.2. But the average index figure for all farm produce was still lower, namely, 86.7. Two years later, when the average index figure for all commodities throughout Canada stood almost exactly at par, 100.1, the figure for all farm produce throughont Canada had risen more rapidly and stood at 96.7. In 1903 the general index figure for all products and the index figure for all farm products had become almost identical, 110.5 for the former, and 110.9 for the latter. By 1907 the index figure for all commodities had mounted to 126.2, but that for agricultural com-

modities to 129.5. The sudden drop in textiles in the
following year, from 126.1 in 1907 to 111.0 in 1908,
brought down the average index figure for all commodities for the year to 120.8, while the figure for
farm products had gone up to 131.1. In 1909, when
the general figure was 121.2, that for agricultural pro-
ductions had grown to 134.9. In 1910 the general
index number reached 124, but the farm index number
had soared to 136.9. In 1911 the figures had become
127.2 for all articles, and 139.4 for the farm's share.
But in the bulletin issued for the month of June, 1912,
when the cost of living throughout Canada, as indicated
by the index number for wholesale prices in general,
had reached the highest point since our records began
to be kept, the highest since our prices were driven
upward by the civil war in the United States, namely
136.9, the average index for all agricultural products
throughout Canada had soared to the incredible height
of 172.7. This is demonstrative evidence that the agricultural base of modern life is with us in Canada insufficient. A greater production on the farm is imperatively demanded for the nation's sake.

Of equally absorbing interest is a detailed comparison of the factors in the cost of living due to the prices
of different classes of goods for the month named, June,
1912. The index figure for beef is an even 200; that
for poultry, 222; for all animals and meats, 178.9;
for all grains and fodders, 189.5; for all dairy products—lowest among produce of the farm—137.4; for
all other foods, 185.3. But the very highest of all
lines apart from farm products is just on a level with
the lowest of these, the index figure for boots and shoes
being 137.9. That for all building materials comes

next, 131.5; for all textiles, 120.7; for drugs and chemicals, 114.4; for housefurnishings of all kinds, 112.8; for all metals and implements, 112.7; for all fuel and lighting, 106.

That the agricultural base of supply in Canada is becoming insufficient, and that a more general production upon the farm is imperatively needed, is shown also by the falling off in the supply of several staple farm products. Canada in 1903 exported to Britain over 34,000,000 pounds of butter. During the last nine months of 1912 this export trade had entirely ceased; not a pound of butter was shipped to Britain. On the contrary, Canada now imports butter from New Zealand. During 1912 we imported in all 5,714,405 pounds, in value amounting to $1,511,654. Of eggs Canada imported during the year, chiefly from the United States, 11,007,345 dozen, paying for them $2,327,924, and paying upon them in customs duties $330,219. Of stall-fed cattle over 45,000 head were shipped from Montreal to Britain in 1911, but less than 6,000 head in 1912. In 1881 there were 3,048,678 sheep upon the farms of Canada; in 1901, 2,510,239; in 1911, 2,106,010. Were we to examine other smaller lines of farm produce we should find the same rule holding good. For instance, we exported in 1912 $6,541 worth of beans, and imported $210,145 worth. Were we to examine the output of each Province we should find the same record. Ontario, for instance, had in 1912 106,000 fewer dairy cattle upon her farms than in 1911. The receipts of fat cattle at the Toronto stock yards fell off from 317,000 head in 1910 to 273,000 head in 1911. Corresponding facts might be cited from every Province and in many fields of out-

FINEST OF FOREST LAND, UNFIT FOR HUSBANDRY.
Here throve the forest primeval; erosion followed removal.

put. A fuller production upon the farm is needed and would bring sure reward.

In the face of such a showing as this concerning relative prices and lowered production, one may well ask in the interest of the general community, " Why is there migration from the farm?" and in the interest of the farmer, " Why is there dissatisfaction with farm life?" The replacing of hand labor by machinery cannot be the sole explanation. Many of our townships had reached their maximum of population before the chief developments in machinery had taken place. Many New England " towns " were becoming depleted as early as the beginning of the nineteenth century. Let us endeavor to search out some of the main causes.

The invariable rule is found to be that depletion shows itself first and works out most completely on the less fertile soils. I have stated that along the nearest concession road to Spencerville, right over against the village, are found seven adjoining farms without a resident farmer. That tract of land is high-lying, stony, thin-soiled over rock, and arid, beyond any adjoining areas. Yet on that now arid territory stumps of pine still remain as evidence of a heavy growth of white pine whose trunks were two and even three feet in diameter.

We thus reach the first of the economic causes of the migration from the farm, due to an error in the field of conservation of natural resources, namely the opening up to settlement and denuding of their forests of lands less profitable for agriculture than for forestry. Lands that are very valuable for forestry may be quite valueless for agriculture. A light soil of limited depth which when cleared washes with the rain, leaving exposed rock, but which is held by binding roots while under forest, is one example. Gravel which parts readily with its water in the open but remains moist when in woods is another. Sand which drifts with the wind is a third. " It is a known fact that in certain upland parts of the Eastern United States the average level of the ground-water has fallen from ten to forty feet . . . while springs and wells have permanently failed."* In their original condition forests throve on these lands. Once cleared it was impossible to maintain conditions under which profitable agriculture could be carried on. Even re-afforesting has become difficult. This condition holds of a large part of the mountainous and hilly districts of the world. Yet upon these districts the waterflow of the streams, and consequently the humidity of the climate, and ultimately the productiveness of all lands depend. Yet the policy of our Governments long fostered exploitation of the forests upon such lands.

A great economic wrong has been inflicted upon the world by the exploitation of all natural resources, a waste made possible by modern means of transportation and manufacture employed under control of the purpose of present gain alone, untempered by the thought of service or of responsibility for the future; a wrong of such magnitude as to amount to actual spoliation of coming generations, of such magnitude as to amount to actual defiance of the God of Providence.

The world of to-day is in the position of an heir who has come into possession of a great estate and is recklessly squandering his patrimony:

Creation's heir, the world, the world is mine.†

* Commission of Conservation, Report I, p. 13.
† Oliver Goldsmith, " The Traveller."

Engineering science has made it possible for men to draw rapidly upon all resources; transportation has made it possible to seize the pristine wealth of all continents, and the foolish heir of the ages has not come to his senses in regard to the use of his new domain.

Men are to-day becoming millionaires through selfish exploitation of forest and stream and field and mine and ocean, and of the toil of their fellow men until not only the blood of the poor innocents, but also the dried-up beds of the brooks, the bared rocks of the hillsides, the weed-covered, scrub-covered fields of our fathers, the shaft-and-tunnel trap-doors of forsaken mines, and the extinct genera of sky and earth and sea cry aloud to God who made all things very good, to the God who "worketh even until now," that He might fashion this earth as a fit habitation for all men of all generations.

I charge our farmers, who go to the West to exploit the virgin fertility of the prairies and have no thought of making a permanent home for themselves or their children there, with a dastardly crime against society; —yet it is a crime in which they are but feeble imitators of the objects of men's worship to-day, the millionaire exploiters of the world's wealth.

Our fathers sinned, both in ignorance and wilfully, and we their children are paying the penalty in depleted communities, but even while paying the penalty we are sinners beyond our fathers.

Yet again, we have other unoccupied farms where substantial buildings, enclosed garden-plots and trim fields, as well as local history, attest the existence of profitable farming carried on in the recent past. Here we reach another error in the realm of conservation— unscientific farming that has depleted the fertility of lands which should have grown in productive capacity under tillage.

Among all recent movements one of the richest promise is that of the national conservation of natural resources. Of these, looked at in their widest range, human efficiency stands first; but next to it, in power for good or ill upon human welfare, undoubtedly ranks fertility of the soil. The Committee on Lands of the Dominion Commission of Conservation carried on in 1911 an investigation in the form of an Agricultural Survey of 1,212 farms throughout the Dominion, 100 in each of the Maritime Provinces, 200 in Quebec, 300 in Ontario, and 412 in the four western Provinces, to discover whether there was upon these farms conservation of fertility, of labor, and of health. The information received was neither second-hand nor superficial. The report of the chairman, Dr. J. W. Robertson, informs us that " In most of the Provinces the farmers are living upon the accumulated capital which nature provided in the soil, leaving their lands poorer because they had been on them."* Yet a fair number are not only maintaining but increasing fertility, and in this fact is found the ground of hope for the future. They are of the type which survives upon the farm, the class to which all shall yet belong. In Prince Edward Island 51 per cent. report larger yields than they had formerly, the increase dating from 15 to 18 years ago. In Nova Scotia 46 per cent. of the farms examined show an increase; in Quebec, 39 per cent.; in New Brunswick and in Ontario 24 per cent., the increase dating from ten years ago, while in Manitoba not one farmer reports

* Commission of Conservation Report, III, p. 57.

an increase, and 46 per cent. acknowledge a marked
decrease. " The decrease of yield per acre in that Province," says Dr. Robertson, " must be concurrent with
exhaustion of fertility."

The broadest inductions we can reach show that this
loss is widespread. The area under cultivation in the
West—Manitoba, Saskatchewan, and Alberta—in-
.creased 269 per cent. in the last decade; the amount of
products increased only 185 per cent. In the United
States the wheat area increased 56 per cent. between
1890 and 1900, the yield only 40 per cent.; the corn
area increased 31 per cent., but the yield only 25 per
cent.

Here again, as in the case of the exploitation of the
forest, the lure of the soil is addressed to the worst that
is in man, the appeal of the soil to his best. " The lure
of the Prairies is like unto the lure of the Yukon and
the lure of the Cobalt,—' Come and take something,
ship it out, and make yourself rich.' " But the
appeal of the soil is that we treat the land with loving
care so as to reap ever-increasing profits while preserv-
ing the crop-producing power of the soil for the benefit
of our descendants. And the reward is not material
only, whether present or prospective. " When man
exhausts the soil, what does he do ? He helps to make
the people more careless and less competent; he leaves
them less power and more poverty in every respect. On
the other hand, when he preserves and increases the fertility of the soil, the people thereby become increasingly
efficient and capable. These two go together. It is
for us to see that the fertility of our soil shall be maintained, and that there shall be continuously improving
conditions for the rural population." " Consider that

report from a virgin Province with the accumulated wealth of 50,000 years of the Creator's deposits in that savings bank of soil; that not one farmer in a hundred has reported any increase over ten years ago, and that 46 per cent. of them have reported a decided decrease. That gives us much food for thought. It brings out a grave situation for consideration. It is to me, much more imminent of blessing or disaster than any other material question now before the West."*

O Demeter, abounding in fruit and ears of the harvest,
Well may this field be wrought and yield a crop beyond
measure.†

But we have not only tracts that are springing up in scrub forest and other areas that afford pasturage for the stock of adjoining farmers; the major portion of the land in the township of Edwardsburg is for sale. Not that it is all so advertised, though much of it is. Leading Edwardsburg farmers assure me that three out of four of the farmers in the township are ready to accept any reasonable offer for their acres. Why should this be the case?

The Lands Committee of the Conservation Commission carried on in 1911 an investigation gleaning information fairly representative of the actual conditions in each Province in regard to the practice of well-planned farming as shown by systematic rotation of crops, the practice of sowing selected seed, and the application of manures; and also as to the inroads of weeds, insect pests, and plant diseases. This inquiry into actual con-

* Report cited, p. 92.
† Theocritus, Idyll X.

ditions was made by competent men. It was scientific research, not in the laboratory, but in the rural community. The Report indicates that a comparatively small number of farms are run under good systems of cropping and good methods of cultivation. A few of the salient points brought out by the survey are: That out of the 800 farms under investigation in the Maritime Provinces, Quebec and Ontario, on only 25 per cent. is any systematic rotation of crops followed; in a representative Ontario county " a percentage of the farmers hardly know what is meant by the term systematic rotation." Yet, Dr. Robertson states, wholly apart from the effects obtained from fertilizers, and simply by the use of a rotation which includes the bean or clover crop, there has been in specified places an increase of from 100 to 150 per cent. in amount, with an increase of from 200 to 300 per cent. in profit.

Mr. Grisdale, Director of Dominion Experimental Farms, stated in his evidence before the Select Standing Committee of the Senate on Agriculture, in 1912, that the average farmer spends $10 an acre in the cultivation of his land, and, according to the census, receives $15.50, making a clear profit of between five and six dollars, but that at the Experimental Farm cultural operations cost $11.77, and crop return is $45.47 per acre, making a profit of $33.70.

As regards the use of selected seed the Report states that by the majority of farmers nothing is done in the way of seed selection more than to grade the grain through a fanning mill. Yet Dr. Robertson assures us that by seed selection alone the crops of Canada can be doubled. " In Ontario, field crops last year were worth $193,000,000, and if there were $193,000,000 more of wealth coined into existence out of chaos, not transferred out of one pocket into another, but called into existence by intelligent labor out of otherwise chaos, indifference, want of knowledge, want of ability, want of application, waste of sun power, and failure to use the seed power that is all about us,—what an enriching gain to us it would be! If the crops of the whole North-west last year—Manitoba, Saskatchewan, and Alberta —had been a complete failure, so that nothing grew, what a depression would have come over Canada, what a measure of dearth and starvation would have come over that part of our inheritance.   That hints at the effect on our national life of $220,000,000 of value from crops being here or not here.   The doubling of the crops of Ontario would be an addition to the value of the crops of Canada almost as great as the addition of the crops of these three great Provinces has been."*

Some years ago Dr. Robertson directed an experiment carried on on 1,400 farms throughout Canada wherein for three successive crops the finest heads were selected from the most vigorous plants of wheat and oats.   The exact amount of increase was computed in percentages. Dr. Robertson, recognized everywhere as one of the world's trusted leaders in reliable experiment, applied the percentage of increase thus obtained to the field crops of Canada, finding that " if all fields had been sown with similarly superior seed, not imported from Kamschatka, but selected from the fields and farms of Canada, we should have got from the same area enough grain to fill 1,500 miles of railway cars ; enough increase above what we harvested to fill 1,500 miles of railway

* Commission of Conservation, Report III, p. 91.

PASTURE ON AN UNOCCUPIED FARM.
Depleted soil, abandoned to the thistle.

cars in one year. Surely that is a confirmation of the statement that if the methods employed by the best 10 per cent. of the farmers prevailed all over Canada, we would get this doubling of the value of our crops, $565,000,000."

The loss from the prevalence of weeds, insects, and plant diseases was found to be heavy. Taking the farmers' own judgment as to the amount of loss—always, when carefully given, an under-estimate because of lack of trained habits of observation—this runs to an average of $75 to $100 to each farm. There are areas in the West actually abandoned through the prevalence of wild oats and stinkweed. In the county of Brome, Quebec, orange hawkweed threatens to destroy the pasture and has reduced its power for carrying stock. In Lanark County, Ontario, the injury done by sow-thistle is so alarming that it is predicted farms will be abandoned. Dr. Robertson remarks, in reporting on this matter: "I do not want to say anything disparaging about Canada . . . but I have to go to Scotland once in a while to get the delight, the refreshing delight to one's eyes, of seeing farming that is clean, and beautiful in its cleanness."

Yet Britain once suffered most severely from weeds. The poet Crabbe gives us this vivid picture:—

> Rank weeds that every art and care defy
> Reign o'er the land and rob the blighted rye;
> There thistles stretch their prickly arms afar
> And to the ragged infant threaten war;
> There poppies nodding mock the hope of toil;
> There the blue bugloss paints the sterile soil;
> Hardy and high, above the slender sheaf
> The slimy mallow waves her silky leaf;

6

O'er the young shoot the charlock throws a shade,
And clasping tares cling 'round the sickly blade;
With mingled tints the rocky coasts abound,
And a sad splendor vainly shines around.*

Loss through inferior stock in dairying is heavy.
The average yearly yield of milk per cow in Ontario
is 4,540 lbs. But there are many cows in the Province
yielding 15,000 lbs., and some that reach 22,000 lbs.
At the Winnipeg meeting of the British Association in
1909 the Danish Live Stock Commissioner described
methods in use in Denmark which had raised the average yield of cows from 80 lbs. of butter in 1864 to 220
lbs. in 1908.

Nor is this the limit of our loss. The township of
Edwardsburg, among other excellent products, yields
potatoes of superlative quality. Competent judges
affirm that at Spencerville Fair the samples of potatoes
annually exhibited grade upon the average higher in
excellence than those seen at the Provincial Exhibition
in Toronto. Yet this superlative crop has no recognized
place in the market. The chief reason appears to be
that a score or two of varieties are commonly grown,
and when shipped all of these varieties may be found
in one carload.

Thus we find that the economic problem is not only
one of technics—of utilizing to best advantage the
powers of nature in growing plants and animals for
human use, but also of economics in its strict sense as a
science—of utilizing agricultural production to best
advantage when it has taken place, through transportation and distribution, through development of consump-

*George Crabbe, " The Village as It Is."

tion, through business co-operation, through all the relations of agriculture to other industries and to legislation.

Dr. George H. Clark, Dominion Seed Commissioner, emphasizes the condition we have just pointed out, as one cause which accounts for the lack of market for products intrinsically good: the absence of standards of uniformity in shipment. " The Ontario potato crop is a badly mixed crop. Were the commercial potatoes that are marketed in Toronto offered in England, London's poor would have an opportunity to buy cheap potatoes. Any good cook will tell you that she gets poor results if she boils long white, round white, and rose types together."*   The same condition and a similar failure are found to apply to the marketing of other products. Successful millers must establish and maintain definite uniform brands of flour. Ontario millers find that they can combine 60 per cent. of Ontario wheat and 40 per cent. of Western wheat with the finest results, yet many of our largest milling concerns are not in the market to buy Ontario wheat, because they find it impossible to get two carloads that will give the same result. Three years ago the Dominion Government advanced 400,000 bushels of seed oats to farmers in the West, owing to the failure of ripened seed in the previous autumn. Ontario had a large supply of good commercial oats to offer ; all were rejected by the Seed Commissioner because obtainable only in mixed varieties and types, The whole amount was secured in Scotland without difficulty, all true to the Abundance type. Mr. Clark asks the farmers of Canada to look at our wheat,

* G. H. Clark, 12th Annual Report, Ontario Agricultural Societies, p. 26.

oats, barley and potato crop through the spectacles of
the miller and the consumer in general, assuring us that
if that be done it will raise the average value of these
crops by several per cent. simply by making the supply
already secured more uniform in quality.

Yet again, potatoes have been delivered on board cars
at Spencerville at thirty cents a bushel, and report says
that the same potatoes have been sold at Toronto, still
on board cars, at a dollar a bushel. That more than
double the amount paid the farmer—whose labor is ex-
pended months in advance, whose capital is engaged
throughout the year—should be paid to the first middle-
man and the transportation company, whose capital is
engaged in this transaction for a few days only, is not
conducive to the satisfaction of the farmer. The cause
of what seems an excessive difference in price would
appear to be due to the fact that farmers are not organized for business purposes. Co-operation is absent.

Too small a proportion of the price paid by the
ultimate purchaser goes to the farmer. Part at
least of the excessive cost of agricultural products
is not due to anything that the farmer does or
leaves undone. According to the United States Department of Agriculture it cost approximately 55
per cent. of what the consumer paid to take the farm
products of that country from the farmer to the consumer. What the farmer sold for six billion dollars
consumers paid thirteen and one-third billions. A Commission appointed by the State of New York reported
lately that the food of New York, as received from the
farmers, costs, laid down at the railway terminals,
$350,000,000 a year, but delivered to the homes
$500,000,000. This added charge of 43 per cent., the

Commission holds, is due in large part, not to excessive profit, but to sheer waste.

There is need of applying business methods to the question of what shall be consumed on the farm and what sent to market. Our exports of farm products constitute a question of supreme national importance. To every hundred dollars' worth of exports from Canada the main industries contribute as follows: Fisheries, $5; manufactories, $12; mining, $15; lumbering, $16; and agriculture, $51. In that proportion do our industries pay our debts to the outside world. Now, some of this agricultural export trade is bad business. " The butter exported from Denmark to Great Britain in 1909 was 197,751,024 lbs., worth $49,802,400; and that almost fifty million dollars' worth of butter carried out of Denmark less of the elements of fertility than did each thousand tons of hay shipped out of Quebec to New England. There is a contrast indeed in the national administration of agriculture! Fifty million dollars' worth of butter impoverishing the land less than each thousand tons of hay, worth at most, $14,000 !"*

Finally, sufficient attention is not paid to sheer excellence of product. In every neighborhood there are a few farmers whose products command a much higher price than those of the majority. " The Danes take from England enough more money than any other nation obtains for an equal quantity of butter, bacon, and eggs, because of their superior quality, to pay for their whole educational work and to have a balance over. For the superiority of their butter, bacon, and

* Conservation Commission, III, p. 103.

eggs, they get, as a premium, more than we spend on our rural schools from the Atlantic to the Pacific."*

Moreover, the farmer bears economic wrongs as well as suffers under economic failure. The report of the Commission on Country Life transmitted by President Roosevelt to the Senate and House of Representatives in 1909 lays the chief emphasis upon this feature of the farm problem. In the view of the members of the Commission the first of the main special deficiencies in country life is " disregard of the inherent rights of the land-worker." The handicaps which they have specially in mind are: the speculative holding of lands, the monopolistic control of means of transportation and of streams; wastage of forests, with consequent exposure to floods and to disastrous soil erosion; and restraint of trade. They find that farm property bears an unjust share in taxation. And among the remedies which they recommend are " a thoroughgoing investigation by experts . . . into the farmer's disadvantages in regard to taxation, transportation rates . . . and credit, . . . and careful attention to the farmer's interests in legislation and the tariff."†

Speculative holding of lands has not as yet become a handicap to farmers in Eastern Canada. But speculative buying of farm lands is a menace of the near future. Throughout New York, Pennsylvania, Ohio, Indiana, and Illinois farm lands have more than doubled in price within a decade. So soon as there is any check upon the freeness of land for settlement in our own West, the conditions which prevail in these States will be found in Canada as well. The rise is speculative in

* The same, p. 104.
† Country Life Commission, Report, p. 8.

character.   There is certainly no legitimate justifica-
tion to be found for it in the relation between investment and return in farming as an industry at present.
The inflation in price would seem to be due to anticipation of a prospective demand for land in the near
future.   Its immediate result is a deceptive prosperity,
and a change in the character of ownership.   The
farmer is able to borrow increased amounts against increased value, and mortgages are increasing; and many
farmers sell at the first slight rise to capitalist investors
who reap the profits of further rise in value, while
tenants replace agricultural owners.   This phase of the
problem is one in regard to which the interest of the
Canadian farmer is expressed in the adage: Forewarned
is forearmed.

But in the West the speculative holding of lands
becomes nothing short of a blight upon progress.
Around railway towns lie concentric circles of vacant
sections.   The townships everywhere are checkered
with unoccupied squares.   The farmer is pressed far
out upon the prairie.   The haulage to the elevator is
increased, and all the conveniences of life lie at a distance.   The making of roads is retarded.   Every mile
of long-distance travel is an economic loss.   The schools
are under a handicap.   The organization of the townships is rendered less effective.

The whole subject of the relation of the great railway systems of Canada to the farmer teems with
questions touching public welfare.   The larger aspect
of several of the questions raised by the American
Country Life Commission are with us embraced under
this head.   The policy followed in opening the West
was controlled more largely by considerations of rail-

way traffic than of common welfare. Settlers were
sought by a world-wide propaganda in order that when
placed on the land they might furnish railway freight-
age. Eventual national progress would have been
more fully secured by a less artificial development.
Agriculture in the West would have developed upon
more helpful lines. It is more than a question whether
agricultural prosperity in the East was not injured
by the forcing of Western grain-growing. The exodus
from Nova Scotia and Ontario was due not only to the
lure of free land in Manitoba, but also to economic
pressure in the East due to artificial development of the
West. And more recently we have seen considerations
of railway haulage become a factor in deciding an
issue of national importance to the disadvantage of the
farmer in the rejection of reciprocity in natural products with the United States. And an injury of great
magnitude has been inflicted upon the farmers of the
West by the exemption of the lands of the Canadian
Pacific Railway Company from taxation. The intention of Parliament was that these lands should be
exempt from taxation until the settlement of the locality; the interpretation placed upon the wording of the
act of gift is that they are exempt until the settlement
of the particular parcel of land. Municipal development and all progress is thereby greatly hampered.

Our system of banking throws an undue burden upon
the farmer. Capital is withdrawn from the country
to be used in the city by means of facilities for making
loans to manufacturers which are denied to farmers.
I have heard farmers object to any proposal to furnish
them with facilities for credit on the ground that such
would be provision for sinking into debt. These indi-

viduals belong to the same economic school as did the
farmer who, when a horse of his was killed, said that
it didn't matter, for the horse had cost him nothing,
as he had paid for him in labor. Credit is one of the
strong factors of modern progress. The farmer needs
it for the utilizing of production in advance of sale.
Too much capital is idle in the hands of farmers.
When the manufacturer has a hundred plows in his
warehouse he can realize upon them at once by bor-
rowing upon them as security. When the farmer has
a thousand bushels of wheat in his granary he cannot
borrow upon it, although it is the best collateral security
in the world. Our banking laws expressly forbid the
banks to make such loans. The farmer must secure
current loans by personal note or by chattel mortgage.
In consequence, although the farmer is the safest of private borrowers, he nevertheless pays the highest rate of
interest. Not in all countries, however. France and
Germany, for instance, have provided adequate farm
credit. And thus, while strong national governments
obtain permanent loans at 2 per cent. interest; while
call loans in New York bear 2.46, and the Bank of
England's discount rate in 1911 averaged 3.47; while
the best commercial paper in New York bears 4.10,
strong railroad bonds 4.60, public utilities 5.00, the
best industrials, 5.50, and average industrials, 6.50;
while French farmers borrow at 4.30, German farmers
at 4.40, and even Arab farmers in Egypt at 8.00, the
American farmer borrows at an average of 8.50 per
cent. Farmers in the Canadian West are charged 10
per cent. by the banks.

Our general system of taxation is an economic injustice to the farmer. All taxation should fall upon value

for production, not upon means of living. To treat all wealth alike in this regard is to fail to see that each generation owns in absolute fee its own production, but has only a life interest in the sources of wealth. There are four factors in production: "land," in its widest economic sense; "labor," including ability as well as toil; capital; and society. The contribution of society is the so-called "unearned increment," which is found not only in the price of land, but in the wages of labor and in the interest of capital. This is the true "unproductive surplus" of political economy. This increment of the value of land, labor, and interest, earned by society, should become, not the subject of taxation, but in its own entirety the whole complement of taxes. The function of taxation is not to lay a burden upon land, labor, or capital, levying the burden according to the patient willingness of the shoulder to bear it, but to appraise the share of production due to society as a partner with the other three and to hand over to her her own. And had society wages as she has worth, wealth would be hers for all her tasks, and her members would be relieved from their burdens alike of poverty and of riches. Under the failure of government to accomplish this true function of taxation the farmer is the chief sufferer. His is the most patient shoulder beneath uneconomic taxation, and upon it in consequence the heaviest load is placed.

Enough! the lie is ended. God only owns the land;
No parchment deed hath virtue unsigned by His own hand,
Out on the bold blasphemers who would eject the Lord,
And pauperize His children and trample on His word.

Behold this glorious temple with dome of starry sky,
And floor of greensward scented and trees for pillars high,
And song of birds for music, and bleat of lambs for prayer,
And incense of sweet vapors arising everywhere.

Behold His table bounteous spread over land and sea,
The sure reward of labor, to every mortal free;
But hark! through Nature's anthem there rises the refrain,
God made the world, but giveth it unto the sons of men.*

* J. W. Bengough, " Verses Grave and Gay."

ECONOMIC SOLUTIONS OF
THE PROBLEM

My lord rides through his palace gate,
My lady sweeps along in state;
The sage thinks long on many a thing,
And the maiden muses on marrying;
The minstrel harpeth merrily,
The sailor ploughs the foaming sea,
    But fall to each whate'er befall,
    The farmer feedeth all.

Smith hammereth cherry-red the sword,
Priest preacheth pure the Holy Word;
Clerk Richard tales of love can tell,
Dame Alice worketh 'broidery well;
Great work is done, be it here or there,
And well man worketh everywhere;
    But work or rest, whate'er befall,
    The farmer feedeth all.
            —*Charles G. Leland.*

————

God, make me worthy of Thy land
  Which mine I call a little while,
  This meadow where the sunset's smile
Falls like blessing from Thy hand,
  And where the river singing runs
  'Neath wintry skies and summer suns.

I would be nobler than to clutch
  My little world with gloating grasp;
  Now, while I live, my hands unclasp,
O let me hold it not so much
  For my own joy as for the good
  Of all the gentle brotherhood.
            —*R. W. Gilder.*

CHAPTER III.

Economic Solutions of the Problem.

Agriculture as a business is advancing. Its rewards to-day are very much greater than ever before. And the efficiency of its service to human need is even greater than the rewards have been.

A comparison of the agriculture of England five hundred years ago with that of the present is informing. " In those days half the arable land lay in fallow. The amount produced was—to take wheat as an example, about eight bushels the acre in ordinary years—less than a third of an average crop at the present time. There were no artificial grasses. Clover was not known, nor any of the familiar roots. As a consequence there was little or no winter feed, except such coarse hay as could be made and spared. Cattle were small, and stunted by the privations and hard fare of winter. The average weight of a good ox was under four hundred-weights. Sheep, too, were small, poor, and came slowly to maturity. The average weight of a fleece was not more than two pounds. With ill-fed cattle there was little or no strong manure. Iron was very dear, costing, to take wheat as a standard of relative value, nine times as much as it does now. But the number of persons engaged in agriculture was nearly as numerous as it now is. It embraced, to be sure, nearly the whole population, though all their labor did not produce an

eighth part of that which is gathered at present."[*]
But great as has been the progress of the art of farming
since the period when the yield was one-eighth of that
now obtained from equal areas of arable land, relatively
to the advance in world progress in general since the
advent of the modern industrial world, agriculture is
falling behind. There has not been the multiplying
of efficiency in this field that there has been in the production of cotton or of steel. Marvellous as has been
the progress in the development of better varieties of
grain—for instance, our new Canadian barley, of
which a recent issue of *World's Work* editorially
says: "Twelve grains of barley have encircled the
earth—twelve grains of barley borrowed from Canada
by the University of Wisconsin have sent millions of
their progeny abroad over our land. Their fame has
made this new race sought even as far as Russia . . .
It has added many millions to the profit of the man on
the soil,"—it has not kept pace with, for example, the
advance in the conquest of disease by modern medical
science. And this relative slackening of pace is much
greater among the main body of agriculturists than
among its leading exponents. The problem of the
farm, from the standpoint of agriculture as an art, is
simply this: how to apply all the elements of modern
efficiency as wrought out in the industrial world as a
whole through invention and organization to that art
throughout its whole extent. Where this is done successfully, as in Denmark, the rural problem is not felt.

So great is this relative failure of farming as an occupation that farm lands have slight value to the farmer

* Thorold Rogers, "Manual of Political Economy," p. 158.

PRIZE FIELD OF OATS, 87 BUSHELS TO THE ACRE. WORLD'S AVERAGE, 28.

Scientific Husbandry Vindicated.

as an investment. They give him little more than opportunity to earn a livelihood as a workman. That is, he receives no " rent," as that term is used in political economy, and little return for capital. The farmer is at once landlord, capitalist and workman. As landlord he owns his land surface. As capitalist he owns his buildings, his stock, his implements, and the tilth in which he keeps his land—all that the farmer in Britain provides, who pays rent for his land-area to the landlord. As workman he fulfils a double function, he is manager of a business and manual laborer. As landlord he is entitled to fair rent as trustee for his land so far as rent does not include unearned special privilege. As capitalist he has the right to the usual reward of capital—and the reward of capital, when its risks also are kept in view, should be fairly equal in all lines of employment. As a workman he is entitled to the wages of labor and of management. The first charge to be paid out of any business is labor's wage, then the wage of superintendence; next comes capital's portion with its two shares, the first for maintenance, the second for interest; and last of all, the portion for rent. Now, in many cases the whole income of the farmer is sufficient only for wages of labor and management, with nothing left as return for the investment of capitalist and landlord. Some fifteen years ago Mr. Robert Sellar, the able editor of the Huntingdon *Gleaner,* made a series of first-hand investigations into the investment and income of farmers in the counties of Chateauguay and Huntingdon, Quebec, and showed conclusively that many received no return, not only as " economic rent," but even for capital invested in equip-

7

ment. This was, indeed, at the period of greatest depression, when farm prices were less than one-half what they are at present. ,But it was also, be it noted, in one of our most fertile districts, the Chateauguay valley, and among a people who rank as one of our progressive farming communities. What was true of such a district at that period must hold even at this time in less fertile districts. The same facts are presented from the obverse point of view by Dr. Warren H. Wilson: " Near Ithica, New York, farmers prosper as they do in few parts of the State, but by a survey made by the College of Agriculture it was found that among 615 farmers the average labor income was only $423. That is, after paying interest on their invested capital and accounting for work done by others the farmer is able to pay himself a wage of only about $1.20 per day."* Nor is this to be considered a trifling item in our national prosperity. A superficial observer might suppose the capital investment of our farmers a bagatelle compared with that in our great transportation, manufacturing and commercial interests. The truth lies quite the other way. Over the Horticultural Building of the Canadian National Exhibition in Toronto in 1912 a streamer was flying bearing the legend: " Ontario's Farmers' Invested Capital One Billion Two Hundred and Fifty Million Dollars." It is vital to Ontario's welfare that that amount be not sunk in unremunerative investment. Ontario's investment in agriculture is greater than all Canada's investment in industrial enterprises. These the *Financial Times* estimates at $1,245,000,000. It is greater than all the

* " Men and Religion Messages," Vol. VI, p. 2.

savings of the people of Canada held as liquid assets. These, as deposited in the banks, amount to slightly over one billion dollars. For every dollar Canada has invested in manufacturing she has five dollars invested in agriculture.

Again, there is a fixed charge against the farm which must be constantly met or farming cannot continue. It is the subsistence wage for the family and cost of wear and tear of the plant. Income from whatever source must meet this of necessity, and more than this for satisfactory living. Beyond it lies the " productive surplus," which makes the business a progressive one, and beyond this again the surplus proper, which constitutes the prize for which progressive industry strives. Suppose this fixed charge to be $750, suppose it $1,000— it varies with the standard of living—if income falls below this amount the alternatives are: to abandon the farm, to live on in grinding poverty, to seek some side line of gain, or—to make farming pay better. The two former alternatives are ruled out for us by our very thesis. Which of the latter is the true alternative ?

Some look for seasonal industries to be established in the country. The demand for farm labor is to some extent a seasonal one ; help is needed at certain times ; there is leisure at others. It is thought that other seasonal industries might be made to dovetail in with this. The hat factories of Brockville and those of Matteawan, New York, call away certain Spencerville people for a time twice a year. Let us, the suggestion runs, have many such seasonal industries in the country itself. I fear the whole scheme is quite utopian. It might serve the other industries slightly ; it could never widely serve the farm home. There is indeed force in Dr. Robertson's words before the Conservation Commission: " A good system of rotation provides for the spreading of the labor of the farmer over most of the year. The other system means a rush of work and very long hours for two months in spring and two in harvest, and little satisfactory occupation during other parts of the year. I have never known a healthy man who, under sixty, could loaf for half the year and escape the devil. I do not mean the devil hereafter, but the devil here and now. A man has to be at something, something with a definite purpose that calls out his powers, or he will not be happy. Where the practicable system of farming does not provide satisfying, profit-leaving work during the winter, let us have what the Swiss have, what the Swedes have: the home industries—not for profits, but for the salvation of the boys and young men, for the satisfaction of the women. Labor, intelligent, skilful labor, labor with good will, is a means of grace, whereby the race will be ever rising, rising, rising."* Dr. Robertson advocates not seasonal industries in factories, but home industries for moral rather than for economic ends. A better way, economically, is the one he points out in his opening sentence. A good system of rotation of crops is the fountain-head of good cultivation, as well as a fountain-head of good living. Of the four economic alternatives the fourth and not the third is the true choice.

Sir Horace Plunkett, who has done so much for Irish agriculture through promoting co-operation, has uttered a famous dictum concerning the needs of

* Conservation Commission, III, p. 96.

American farmers: "Better living, better farming, better business." Now it is as often better business as it is better farming that is necessary for the better living that is sought. Just as the weakness, economically, of the factory worker lies in this, that the capitalist, who holds the stronger economic position, controls the whole product, produced co-operatively by capitalist and laborer, so the economic weakness of the farmer lies in this, that he has no voice in fixing the price for which he sells his products, no voice in fixing the cost of transport for his products, and no voice in fixing the price of the commodities required in his occupation; and also in that whereas his market has become world-wide, and the unit of sale has become the carload, he has no means whereby he can sell by sample at a distance, or furnish products by the unit of delivery. The farmer must enter the modern brotherhood. The repair of country life can only come on modern lines. Nevermore can we have the independent household unit or the self-sufficient farmstead any more than we can have the journeyman days of industry restored. The efficiency of agriculture calls for organization and specialization corresponding to those which have made modern industry productive.

The rural problem is far from being solely, or even chiefly, an economic one. But in so far as economic in character it must have an economic remedy. Counsels of patience avail naught here, and the rewards of gracious growth under discipline are the incentives in another realm of struggle than this. Yet the economic remedy is found to have, at every step of its application, a moral implicate without which it is unavailing and unavailable. What is needed is a new rural organization whose formative processes themselves shall prove to be at once the needed ethical disciplines which shall bring the new age into touch with God through Christ and the social opportunities for the satisfaction of aspirations now unrealized.

All lands must be put to their best use. In Edwardsburg we have several thousands of acres of sand-barrows. Once they had mould enough to yield large crops of corn, rye and potatoes. Now they afford scanty pasture. So soon as the mould is once broken through they become drifting sand. There are already many hundreds of small areas where the sand drifts in wavelets with every wind. It is beautiful, but with a beauty which is costly and is unappreciated. The fertile intervales between the sand-barrows are threatened. Herein lies a real community danger.

For years past I have urged, from every available platform, the instant duty of reafforesting every acre where drift may yet occur. Last year I was invited by a farmer in the neighboring township of Augusta to visit his farm and see a plantation of four thousand thrifty young pine trees from one to four years old, growing where drifting sand had been. The Government of Ontario had supplied the seedlings free of charge. It is the beginning of much that is yet to be. Forestry, silviculture, shall yet rank with agriculture. Its importance as an occupation, to say nothing of its importance in conserving stream flow, rainfall, fertility, and climate, or in supplying the world's timber needs, is not realized. " For example, in our Province of British Columbia the timbered land will have 10,000 to 40,000 feet of timber to the acre, say on an average 25,000 feet, which would furnish to our transportation companies material for freight to the extent of 37½ tons. If the land were used for agricultural purposes it would take the crops for fifty years to equal this. In marketing this crop of timber there would be spent in wages only over five dollars per thousand feet, or $125 per acre; and the Government would receive fifty cents per thousand feet, or $12.50 per acre as royalty. How many years of cultivation for agricultural purposes would it take to produce the same result?"* "To cite another case of financial result of forest management, I may refer to waste-land planting in France, which was carried on with State aid by municipalities and private enterprise. Here, in the last sixty years, 2,300,000 acres of absolute waste land of various descriptions were reclaimed by forest planting at a total cost of $15,000,000. These areas are now estimated to be worth $135,000,000, and furnish annual crops valued at $10,000,000, or, in other words, yield 67 per cent. on the initial outlay."† When waste land is allowed to return to forest without care the result is scrub growth. The forest of silviculture is as different from such woods as are the fields of the College at Ste. Anne from those of the Syrian peasant. Let me cite one other example of actual attainment, from Massachusetts. Three-year-old plants of Norway spruce were set out in 1878 on hillsides, in poor sandy soil, unfit for cultivation, which was yielding less than fifty cents per acre yearly as pasture. The land cost the State five dollars per acre. In 1910 four average trees were cut for wood-pulp. They ran from 56.7 to 71.8

* John Hendry, Commission of Conservation, II, p. 93.

† Dr. B. E. Fernow. The same, I, p. 32.

feet in height and from 0.9 to 1.3 feet in diameter at the base. The four trees gave 70.6 cubic feet of timber for pulp, which yielded 1,225 lbs. of the dry product. At the present price of pulp the total yield per acre, if cut, would be $1,111. If to the value of the land an equal sum be added for the planting, plus compound interest and taxes, the total capital employed may be estimated at $64.83 per acre, so that the total yield for 32 years would be $1,046, or $32.70 per acre for each year.* All hillsides and all rough lands in the world should be in forest.

A few miles from Spencerville stands a shaft on the spot where the first MacIntosh apple tree grew. In its native home, Eastern Ontario, this fine variety attains an excellence which it reaches nowhere else; and here it should be largely grown. The orchard lands of British Columbia command a price of $1,000 an acre. Yet large areas in our Eastern Provinces— those adapted to the growing of the MacIntosh in Eastern Ontario, for instance, the Fameuse near Montreal, or the New Brunswicker in the St. John Valley—are in the market for one-tenth to one-twentieth or even one-fortieth of that price because now devoted to dairying and grain-growing, which under scientific orcharding would yield as large returns as do the Okanagan fruit lands. Not over one-tenth of the suitable land is under orchard in the far-famed Annapolis Valley.

Putting the land to a more appropriate use has proved, in specific cases, a real solution of the problem of depopulation. Fruit-growing has saved the situation in several counties in Ontario. Wentworth County

* Publications of the International Agricultural Institute, Rome, Vol. I, No. 6, p. 34.

FRUIT LANDS, GRIMSBY, ONTARIO.

Adaptation of soil to best use secures social strength and economic growth.

is one of the ten Census Districts with a growing rural population. Let us take Saltfleet, one of its townships, as an illustration of our principle. This is a lakeside, fruit-growing township. After a temporary decline in population between 1881 and 1891, it has grown from 2,765 in 1891 to 3,029 in 1901, and 4,458 in 1911, an increase of 61 per cent. in twenty years; while Binbrook, lying just behind it, with ordinary agriculture, declined from 1,674 in 1891 to 1,403 in 1901, and 1,245 in 1911, a decrease of 25 per cent. in the same period. The County of Lincoln is another of the growing districts. North Grimsby is an example of its fruit-growing townships, increasing in rural population from 1,095 in 1891 to 1,321 in 1901, and 1,758 in 1911, a growth of 60 per cent. in a score of years; while South Grimsby, immediately adjoining, declined, with mixed farming, from 1,610 in 1891 to 1,379 in 1901, a loss of 14 per cent. in ten years, but which with the adoption of orcharding has again begun to hold its own. In each of the ten growing districts—in all of which there had been a previous decline of population— there has been adoption of some line of special agriculture.

Another point of exceeding interest is to be noted in this connection. The class that is growing is always the one which is rendering fullest service to the community, not the one which is taxing it most severely. Such is the case with the fruit-growers of Canada in comparison with her general farmers. In 1911, when the average index figure for farm products in general stood at 139.4, for all fresh native fruits it stood at 116.1, with a drop in the summer fruit season to 89.1. The average figure for the decade has been only 107.

But forestry and orcharding touch merely the fringe of the application of this principle of adapting the system of farming to the nature of the land.   An analysis of the soil of the Red River Valley, made at Rothamsted, in England—where soils are known as nowhere else—reveals that the plains of Manitoba, the objective point of the migrations of the buffalo of old, are best suited to grass.   And grass, plain grass, is king; and neither wheat nor corn nor cotton.   Grass conserves, protects, enriches the soil.   Grass in abundance spells good crops for years to come.   Grass is the foremost crop in extent, the greatest revenue producer of the world.   It, too, in turn, needs to be adapted to fittest use.   In Lanark County, Ontario, Drummond, with level, rich soil and good roads, is best fitted for dairying; Dalhousie, with rolling hills and fertile valleys, is the natural home of beef cattle, while Burgess, with its large, rougher farms, is an ideal home for sheep.

Adaptation to soil, climate, and all conditions, must become the fundamental condition of all husbandry. An American authority puts the case well: " In a rough way the American farmer has done precisely this.   The wheat belt, the corn belt, the cotton belt, the sugar-beet belt, the fruit belts, are the result of this adaptation.   In the future, however, an approximate or rough adaptation will not answer.   It must be accurate, scientific.   The number of cultivated crops is sure to increase rapidly.   New varieties will demand special environment.   Competition between lands will force the best use of every acre.   Minute conditions of soil-texture, slope, drainage, rainfall, frost-line, sunshine,

are already considerations in intensive farming, and
will dominate more and more widely."*

But how secure this? Leading farmers everywhere
are already guided by it; how shall all be led to follow?
Such is the final question in all discussions of our
problem. The solution is not economic in nature, but
ethical—it depends not on knowledge, but character.
" The results of intellectual achievement of one race
or one man may be freely borrowed by the rest of the
world, provided the rest of the world have the moral
qualities which will enable them to profit by them;
whereas moral qualities cannot be borrowed by one race
from another. Japan, for example, could easily borrow
from European nations the art of modern warfare,
together with its instruments of destruction; but did
not borrow, and could not borrow, that splendid courage
and discipline which enabled her to utilize so efficiently
the inventions which she borrowed. So one nation can
easily borrow farm machinery and modern methods of
agriculture, but it cannot borrow the qualities which
will enable it to profit by them. Saying nothing of
mental alertness and willingness to learn, . . . it
could not borrow that patient spirit of toil, nor that
sturdy spirit of self-reliance, nor that forethought which
sacrifices present enjoyment to future profit, nor can it
borrow that spirit of mutual helpfulness which is so
essential to any effective rural work, . . . nor can
it borrow a general spirit of enterprise which ventures
out upon plans and purposes which approve themselves
to the reason. These things have to be developed on

* K. L. Butterfield, " Country Church and Rural Problem,"
p. 14.

the soil, to be bred into the bone and fibre of the people;
and they are the first requisite for good farming."*
These considerations apply to every successive requisite
for betterment, and make the problem fundamentally
a problem for the church.

Care, too, for the conservation of fertility, we must
have. Canada apparently ranks fairly well in production per acre. Measured by yield of wheat, our
average per acre in 1911 was 19.5 bushels, whereas that
of Russia was 8, of the United States 12.6, of France
20.5 bushels. Yet our standing in productiveness is
only apparent. We seem to be doing fairly well
because we are bringing virgin land by the million
acres under crop, thus keeping average up. But how
does even that average compare with Britain's 32.6 or
Denmark's 44.8 bushels to the acre?

Our fresh-turned prairie sod affords a yield above
Europe's best. What would it not mean to us if such
fertility were maintained? And it could well be. The
pity of the present situation, with rapid depletion of
fertility, is that it is quite unnecessary. Not only so,
but fertility once lost can be restored. Two hundred
years ago the yield of wheat in England was eight
bushels to the acre. During the last fifty years it has
averaged from thirty to forty bushels. The possibilities for Ontario, whose average in 1910 was 25.2 bushels
for fall wheat, and for spring wheat 20.19 bushels,
is shown by yields obtained at the Experimental Farm
at Guelph. Fourteen varieties of wheat which had
been under test for sixteen successive years gave in 1911
an average yield of 50.5 measured bushels of 62.2 lbs.

* Prof. T. N. Carver, " Rural Economy a Factor in the Success of the Church," p. 15.

to the bushel and for the sixteen-year period an average of 46.7 bushels averaging 61.3 pounds per bushel. A four years' rotation was employed. A light application of barnyard manure was made once in each rotation. No artificial fertilizers were used.

So great a physicist as Sir William Crookes feared that there was danger that the nitrogen of the soil might be too scant for producing permanently sufficient wheat crops. But through the discoveries of later investigators we have learned that by means of the life of bacteria on the roots of clover, alfalfa, and all legumes, nitrogen is taken directly from the air and prepared for the use of other plants. There are only three factors in depletion of fertility—the loss of humus; the decrease of either of three inorganic elements, nitrogen, potash, and phosphorus; and deficiency of bacteria. All three factors are easily controlled; the presence of any one is most serious. On our prairies, humus, so abundant in the virgin sod, is being lost so rapidly that the spring winds blow away the soil, leaving the seed exposed. The rotation of two crops and fallow must be replaced by a rotation including grass or clover. "Experiments in Minnesota have shown that out of 170 lbs. of nitrogen lost from virgin soil in a year only 27½ were absorbed by the crop and 132½ were purely and simply lost. The only means known whereby such loss can be prevented is to alternate the raising of wheat with crops of vegetables and of forage." Dr. Frank T. Shutt, of the Dominion Experimental Farm, by means of analyses which rank among the most thorough-going ever made on this continent, has shown that there is only nitrogen enough in the best soils of Canada for 150 crops of cereals, but over each acre floats in the air enough for a million crops, upon which we may draw by means of clover. Potash is liberated through fermentation by the use of manure. But Dr. Robertson's words are to be well weighed when he tells us that " phosphorus is somewhat deficient; and there is great danger for the future of farming in Canada unless we conserve that and put it back upon the soil."* As to the third factor in depletion, we know that " by cultivation and good management the farmer can increase the population of his soils by many myriads of bacteria per square inch in the course of a few years."† Yet I have seen in Ontario fields of loam where heavy crops of rye had been recently grown, lying uncultivated and in such shape that upon more than two-thirds of the surface of the soil no weeds were to be seen. The ground was bare. Bacteria there were almost none in that soil.

In my judgment this is almost the chief economic cause of the rural exodus. Few think of leaving the farm whose crops are increasing. And here again the implications of the problem are ethical. The brief history of the North Dakota Better Farming Association brings this fact out clearly. Although that State, the pristine richness of whose prairies was so great, was settled only in 1880, the average yield of wheat from 1905 to 1910 was but 12 bushels to the acre. In 1911 it fell to 9 bushels. Thereupon Mr. A. Rogers, the lumber king of the State, sought out Mr. B. L. Howe, the elevator king, and said, " This State is going back to the badgers. We have not more than ten years' business ahead of us." Together they called on Mr. J. J.

* Conservation Commission, III, p. 62.
† The same, p. 48.

Hill, who from his desk reached for a paper in a pigeonhole, saying, " Here is your plan for betterment, and here is a subscription of $5,000 a year for three years to put it through." The Soo line of railway and the Great Northern each duplicated his gift. The banks, townships, and the counties contributed, until there was in hand the sum of $43,000 a year for three years. The Association sent to the Minnesota State Agricultural College begging the loan of their best man for three years as Director. Professor Thomas N. Cooper was sent. By spring fourteen counties were organized under a force of twenty-six men whose work was to give practical demonstrations in the field, and teach rotation of crops and farm accounting. At the close of the first season's work, Professor Cooper tells the Better Farming Association that what they must get after first is not the betterment of North Dakota's wheat or flax crop, but her Man crop. The problem is one of character.

The church must teach that conservation is a moral task; must sound a clear note against exploitation of the soil as essentially immoral. Farmers know familiarly the common practice of tenants whereby a course of cropping is pursued that will take the utmost possible out of the land within the rental period. They recognize that it is to the disadvantage of the owner, but they look on him as helpless. The church must stress the Old Testament truth, never to be superseded, that the earth is Jehovah's. God is that Owner whose fields men are devastating, and He is not helpless in the case. Such preaching, listened to, will hold men on the land through their prosperity, and to their blessedness.

There must be adaptation of farm practice, along all lines, to scientific methods of production. What does not the world owe to men such as Lord Townshend, to whom is attributed the famous Norfolk four-year rotation of crops; Robert Bakewell, who in England in the eighteenth century adopted the methods by which all breeds of live stock have since been improved; Sir J. B. Lawes, of Rothamsted, who taught men to understand the soil; and Luther Burbank, of Santa Rosa, who has raised the development of vegetable life to a new plane! Similar work is being done most successfully in Canada. The technicists of the Dominion Experimental Farms " have given the farmers of the West control over the climate to the extent of escaping frosts in great measure by means of varieties of wheat which will ripen days earlier than was formerly the case." The technicists of the Ontario Agricultural College have given to the world a barley which yields on the average some four bushels to the acre more than any other variety before grown. At Macdonald College at Ste. Anne de Bellevue, Quebec—the Agricultural Department of McGill University—experimental and educational work is being carried on over a square mile of farm land, which is the equal of any being done in the world. From these sources and from many others, through our Farmers' Institutes and other organizations, we obtain every needed help for a great forward movement. President Butterfield, of the Agricultural College of Massachusetts, generously acknowledges our standing: " Ontario presents a good illustration of how a good agriculture can be created in a dozen years, by co-operating methods of agricultural education. Her provincial department of agriculture, her experimental

LOADS OF GRAIN FROM EQUAL PLOTS, WITH CLOVER AND WITHOUT.

The value of crop rotation demonstrated.

station, her agricultural college, her various forms of extension work, and her various societies of agriculturists have all worked together with an unusual degree of harmony for the deliberate purpose of inducing Canadian agriculturists to produce the things that will bring the most profit. The results have been most astonishing and most gratifying."* To read such words may bring a glow of satisfaction. But let not the satisfaction obscure for us the force of the wise words. Agriculturists need to be *induced* to produce the things that will bring most profit. Again we meet with the ethical implication of the economic remedy. Duty is laid upon the progressive man and unprogressive alike. How shall we gain what Denmark has found? No farmer to-day in Denmark feels that he has done his duty, if he has discovered a better method of raising a crop or feeding a cow, until he gets all others to adopt the same method. How shall others realize that " agriculture is for the gaining of crops, and the gaining of the best crops from a constantly improving soil depends upon the capacity and quality of the men "? Whence the " statesmanship in agriculture which shall ensure the perpetual well-being of an intelligent people animated by goodwill and rooted in land well tilled and beautiful? That, I think, might be to us a vision, as it should be an incentive to help in the making of the new earth wherein dwelleth righteousness."†

And there must come adaptation of farm management to the most improved methods of modern business. A Spencerville farmer was transformed from a routine

* K. L. Butterfield, " Chapters in Rural Progress," p. 190.
† Dr. J. W. Robertson, Commission of Conservation, I, p. 59.

8

worker into an alert business man by the introduction
of the Babcock test in dairying.   Its use revealed to
him that he kept a few cows at good profit, and yet
more at no profit.   He began to apply the same business
principle to other things—the feed value of different
fodders, for instance.   Then accurate records of the
daily production of milk by each cow in the herd were
begun.   Pedigreed stock of the finest strains was purchased, and developed with unusual success.   Some
time ago a stockman visited his barn, examined his
records, picked out a score of head, and asked, " What
is your figure for these ?"   When, after computation,
the farmer named his figure, the stockman without a
word wrote out a cheque for the amount.   The sum
was larger than all the stock of every kind upon the
farm, together with all the equipment of the farm,
together with a fair proportion of the price of the farm
itself, had amounted to fifteen years before.   What had
business methods meant to that farmer ?   He had
learned to make a livelihood ; but more, he had learned
to live.   He and every member of his family had found
in farming a zest unknown before.   It had become an
absorbing occupation, and thereby many of the interests
of life had been transformed.   Those who begin to live
in this way do not leave the farm.   There are many
particulars concerning which there is a clamant cry
for the application of better business to farm management, but in no particular is the need more pressing
than in providing some more efficient means of distribution of farm products.   There exists a small co-operative association of farmers at Spencerville who ship
their eggs under guarantee of freshness, uniformity of
size and color, and regularity of supply, and gain from

two to ten cents a dozen above the regular price by doing
so. A farmer had a fairly good two-acre orchard from
which he received about $75.00 a year for his fruit.
A co-operative society was formed in the neighborhood
in 1906. He joined it for the purpose of setting an
example rather than for any particular good that he
thought he would receive at the hands of the Association. But improving influences were at work, and
year by year this improvement was measured by his
returns. In 1911 the same man with the same orchard
and practically the same number of ·trees received
$432.00 for his apples. The co-operative packing,
under positive guarantee, of the apples of British
Columbia has gained for them a market and fame. The
St. Catharines Cold Storage and Forwarding Company
is an example of what can be done in the shipping of
produce. Their distributions have grown from a few
hundred dollars in the first year to $90,000 in 1911,
and upon this it is safe to say that there has been a saving of between $10,000 and $20,000 in the year to the
farmers. The company is co-operative. The Canadian
Seed-Growers' Association is a fine example of the improvement of the conditions of an industry possible
under co-operation.

Sir Horace Plunkett, one of the ablest of the writers
who have discussed on its economic side the farm question as it exists in the United States, regards this as the
first essential in meeting the problem: " The Country
Life movement deals with what is probably the most
important problem before the English-speaking peoples
at this time. Now the predominance of the towns,
which is depressing the country, is based partly on a
fuller application of modern physical science, partly on

superior business organization, partly on facilities for occupation and amusement; and if the balance is to be redressed the country must be improved in all three ways. There must be better farming, better business, and better living. These three are equally necessary, but better business must come first. For farmers, the way to secure better business is co-operation, and what co-operation means is the chief thing that the American farmer has to learn."* Such business co-operation the farmers of Denmark have secured, and in securing it have become strong. By means of it the farming of Denmark is so specialized and so organized that it resembles more the great modern industries than old-time farming. Yet the land is still owned and worked by small-acreage farmers. In no other country is farm population holding its own as in Denmark.

The first requisite for such co-operation in Canada is the securing of legislation authorizing the formation of co-operative societies, defining their objects, powers and responsibilities, and providing safeguards for their operation and for central co-ordinating societies. There is an essential difference between the organization requisite for joint stock companies and co-operative societies, a difference indicated by the very names of the two classes of organizations. The one is a combination of capital, the other an association of persons. In the control of the company the holding of shares constitutes the voting power; in the control of the society membership does so.

Sir Horace Plunkett says: " The object of rural associations is not to declare a dividend, but to improve

* Sir Horace Plunkett, " The Rural Life Problem in the United States," p. 84.

the conditions of the industry for the members. In the control of the management the principle of ' One Man One Vote ' should be strictly observed, an essential condition of co-operative as distinguished from joint-stock organization."* " This principle is so well established by the experience of all countries that it is rather remarkable that it has not yet affected Canadian legislation. Those who have read the history of co-operation will have remarked that while there are individual societies composed of men of exceptional ability and public spirit that have succeeded with a joint-stock organization, yet speaking generally co-operation has been a dismal failure until suitable legislation was provided, or at least until antagonistic laws have been repealed."† As our legislation now is, Canadian farmers seeking formal organization are obliged to use the methods of capitalism that enable those whose interests are not necessarily in the land or the industry to control the organization and take what toll they please.

But more than legislation is required. Law is effective only as it embodies public will. In 1896 the National Agricultural Union of Great Britain attempted co-operation on a large scale. The British Produce Supply Association was formed. A quarter of a million dollars was put in the scheme. Owing, however, to the want of organization among the farmers it was found that regular supplies could not be obtained. How shall the co-operative spirit be fostered? Here as everywhere, we come finally to the moral difficulty underlying the economic one. Our farmers' boys do not

* *The Outlook*, December, 1911.

† A MacNeil, Department of Agriculture, Canada, " Report, Third Conference of the Fruitgrowers of Canada," p. 19.

learn team-play in their games at school, and the lack follows them throughout life. A spirit of independence is the strength but becomes the weakness of rural life. Bishop Gruntvig's splendid Folk Schools scattered broadcast the seeds of co-operation throughout Denmark. The Roman Catholic Church, under Leo XIII., deliberately adopted similar methods in the Encyclical " Rerum Novarum," and the fruit is being seen in the " Catholic Workmen's Organizations " of Europe. Is there not a lesson here for us?

Co-operation in Canada has so far been found in two classes of farm industry only, dairying and fruit-growing. It is equally applicable to stock-raising and to all forms of farm production. It is the needed agency for securing all the desiderata mentioned in our previous discussions,—transportation, distribution, development of markets, selling by sample, uniform grading of products, and excellence of output.

But co-operation has still another field of operation in the farmer's relation to the financial world. We have a fine example of what can be accomplished in this direction in co-operative insurance in the Grenville Patrons' Mutual Fire Insurance Company. Its office is in the village of Spencerville; the directors are all farmers of the vicinity. It is now in its twenty-first year of service. Its operations extend over five counties. The policies in force number 4,957, their average amount $1,600; the amount at risk $7,916,460. The business has been carried on with unbroken and increasing success from its inception. Such co-operative financial concerns are an earnest of what our farmers will yet accomplish.

At the beginning of the present session of Parliament the Hon. C. W. White promised that the Bank Act would undergo amendment during the session authorizing banks to make loans on the products of the farm, even including live stock. There are hints that opposition has arisen and that the bill will be withdrawn. Such an outcome would constitute a call to our farmers to form co-operative banking associations. There may be other reasons for such action. Our banking system is highly centralized. There are but five and twenty banks in Canada. Two dozen bank managers control the available liquid savings of the Dominion. It might prove in the interest of national well-being that another system of banking should arise to offset such centralization.

Germany has a highly effective form of rural co-operative banking. In 1847 F. Raiffeisen, Burgomaster of Flammersfeld, finding that the farmers of his district could borrow only at usurious rates, formed co-operative unions of the better-off citizens to loan to the poorer. No profit was sought. The principle was disinterested love. After fifteen years, Raiffeisen confessed failure; unions based on this principle had no vitality. He then formed co-operative loan banks. Farmers in a defined district syndicate their farm lands under negotiable bonds which are offered jointly as security for the credit the society needs. The individual farmer then borrows from this society. The Central Co-operative Bank of Prussia co-ordinates the societies. The source-book for information upon their working is Volume I., Monographs on Agricultural Co-operation, the International Institute of Agriculture, Rome. There are over 16,000 of the co-operative societies, united in fifty-two federations, all united in the Central Co-operative Bank. Their loans to farmers in 1910 amounted to $3,800,000,000. The average rate of interest paid by farmers is 4.4 per cent. They form the foundation on which the whole structure of co-operation in Germany is built. Never, even during the stress of the Franco-Prussian war or the later agricultural depression, has there been the failure of a single one. A Commission appointed by President Taft recommends their adoption in the United States. The Raiffeisen system has improved social conditions. Our mortgage system lowers them. In Germany the directors are the borrower's neighbors. To them he must explain his need of money and his hope of repayment. When an intemperate man is given a loan after promising to leave drink alone it is to the interest of his neighbors to keep him sober. German pastors affirm that the Raiffeisen system is one of the strongest moral influences in the community.

It is, finally, through the adoption of the co-operative principle that we shall at length attain the political unity and efficiency of rural communities so greatly needed—not for class legislation, which is only evil continually—but for rendering forever impossible class legislation hostile to the farmer, and for linking in one upward movement of civilization the forces of reform in city and country,

In building up our Northern Land to be
A vast Dominion stretched from sea to sea,
A land of labor but of sure reward,
A land of corn to feed the world withal,
A land of life's rich treasures, plenty, peace,
Content, and freedom both to speak and do,—
A land of men to rule with sober law
This part of Britain's empire, next the heart,
Loyal as were their fathers, and as free!*

* William Kirby, " Canadian Idylls," p. 136.

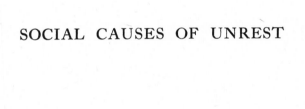

SOCIAL CAUSES OF UNREST

Would I, too, were a man like Philippo
To mount, and lover-like, in boots and spurs,
Rush into the great city's open arms!
The country is a dull old-fashioned maid,
Well enough, truly, for young wayward children,
As is a spinster aunt to care for them.
But when those children are grown men and women
They will be governed by the aunt no more!
I'm weary of these grave environing woods
'Midst which I dwell and watch e'en wandering clouds,
Until I yearn to wander after them.
                                    —*J. A. Middleton.*

CHAPTER IV.

A better rural life must indeed be based on rural economic prosperity. But the problem is not fundamentally an economic one. Dr. Josiah Strong, " whose inspiring and thorough social studies opened to men this field of observation," has ever urged this. The problem of production has been solved, he considers. Let us suppose, he adds, the problem of distribution (that is, the adjustment of wealth, not the transport of products) also solved, so that there should be ample provision assured for the physical wants of every human being for all time to come. Would people, he then asks, would people, delivered from the fear of poverty, be more satisfied with life, more devoted to each other? This question he answers by asking another: Has this beatific, altruistic change taken place in our wealthy class who are freed from thought of reach of want? James Russell Lowell in his last address to college students bade them never forget the reason for which colleges exist: " Not that you may get something by which to earn your bread, but that every mouthful of bread may be more sweet to your taste." The rural problem is very largely one of such appreciation of life.

The problem of production is far from being solved. In Canada we have wheat in abundance, and therefore bread, though bread alone, of our necessary food, keeps low in price. But we have not the fruit nor flesh nor

123

fish nor fowl we need. The fear of famine for the
world is past, but the dawn only is breaking of that
bright morning when the earth shall yield her increase.
The whole wide earth shall yet become one great garden
of God, fertile and beautiful.

Reclamation shall yet take place by irrigation of
millions of acres now thought worthless, and of other
millions by drainage; rich bottom lands shall be pro-
tected from river overflow by levees, and dykes reclaim
the fertile silt of lake and sea.

Conservation of soils from erosion, conservation of
the fertility of soils and of the means of enrichment of
soils, conservation of streams and forest and climate,
shall become universal; and the woods crowning all
the hillsides shall be peopled with plumaged birds and
fur-clad animals yielding regulated tribute to man.

The work of the wizards of agriculture in the development of grains, grasses, roots and fruits, shall go
on until every vegetable product shall exceed present
standards as far as the apples of Annapolis surpass the
wayside crab.

The work being done by national commissions in
searching all lands for every plant and shrub and vine
and tree suited to the climatic conditions of other countries shall become universally successful until each
country shall find itself, as John Reade has sung of
Canada:

> Binding the charms of all lands that are rarest,
> Like the bright cestus of Venus, in one.*

All that is best in each national system of agriculture—the patient labor of China, where even now no

* John Reade, " The Prophecy of Merlin."

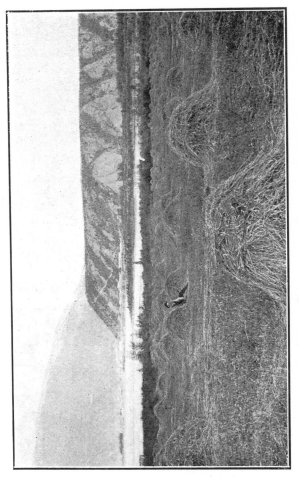

HAYFIELD ON THE KLONDYKE, SUB-ARCTIC.

The heritage of "Our Lady of the Snows."

weed is ever seen—the universal proprietorship of
France, the technical research of Germany, the scientific cultivation of Britain, the progressive management
of America, the thorough co-operation of Denmark,
shall become the heritage of all.

And then shall the earth yield her increase.   The
Sahara shall become an unroofed greenhouse, arcaded
with palms, garlanded with vines, swarded with gourds;
every mile of the tropics shall be pruned into exuberant
largesse, and even the Arctics shall yield a richer tribute
than temperate zones once gave—for it is a scientific
fact that the moss-covered tundras of our Northland,
when once our herdsmen tend the reindeer there, are
fitted to give as rich an output of food for man as do
the grassy plains of Texas with their long-horned steers
to-day.

Let none despise the heritage of Our Lady of the
Snows!   Why do the wild birds migrate to the north?
Not for longer hours of daylight, and not for solitude
for nesting, but for ampler food-supply.   Lean of sinew,
they fly high above our ken as they go north, and the
pot-hunter scarce deigns to look for them as they pass.
Rotund of body, they fly low as they return, and are
everywhere slaughtered, for they have fed fat upon the
myriad swarms of insects of the Arctic summer, and
their very flesh is stained purple with the juices of the
berries of its autumn.   Why are our shoals of finest
food-fishes, why the whale, nature's masterpiece of physical growth, denizens of the cold waters only?   Because the cold waters, and they alone, are literally thick
with food.   And man shall yet, in some way, follow
nature's hints; and when he shall begin to tend his
flocks of solan geese and eider duck, he shall ask, but

ask in vain, Why did not our fathers conserve for us the musk-ox, and all the wild one-time denizens of this world of God's and ours?

The problem of production, now being solved as regards girders and rivets, shall then be solved as regards bread for a fuller world. Shall it be a satisfactory and a satisfied world? That will be found to depend on whether all that is best in every system of agriculture in amplest development, and in every form of industry, shall be crowned by the Christian ideal of service to humanity—on the degree to which our struggling democracy shall be transformed into the likeness of the kingdom of God.

The farmer has been dissatisfied with his returns. But he is even more discontent with his situation. He finds his conditions of labor unsatisfactory, his means of education and recreation, his home, and even his church. The country is lacking in the joy and pride of labor; it is lacking in social life at present, though it remembers wistfully the social pleasures of the past; lacking in a system of education adapted to the farm, as our present school system is fitted to prepare for the business office or the university; it is lacking in healthful recreations, in appreciation of country values; lacking in community ideals, in altruism, in all the newer ethical implications and applications of religion. And, inasmuch as man cannot live by bread alone, even were there no economic problem, people would still leave the country.

The hours of labor are long upon the farm. A fortnight ago I was a guest over night at a farm home. Though I was downstairs at a quarter past six in the morning breakfast was already over. My hostess apologized, explaining that the men must have breakfast before they began their day's work. " But surely," I said, " that compels you to be at work very early in preparing their meal for them before their work begins." " I am up every morning at half-past four," was her reply. Yet it had been almost eight in the evening when, the day's work being over, we three had sat down to the feast of reason, the flow of soul, and the joy of the spirit. The Federal Council of the Churches of Christ in America has adopted a platform which has been styled the social creed of the churches and hailed as the magna charta of the worker's sacred rights. This social creed asserts that the churches must stand " for the gradual and reasonable reduction of the hours of labor to the lowest practicable point, and for that degree of leisure for all which is a condition of the highest human life." The Pittsburg Survey declared not only the seven-days week of labor, but the twelve-hours day in vogue among the steel-workers, a disgrace to civilization. What of the sixteen-hours day of many of our women on Canadian farms? The hours are long for others than women. The growing boy, the immature youth, should not be expected to plod along as steadily as the mature man, even through the rightful hours of well-regulated toil. Forgetfulness of this on the part of the father is the cause of much dissatisfaction among country boys. And worse even than forgetfulness may be found. There are undoubtedly cases upon the farm where parents exploit their children's labor for the sake of the money return as really as do employers of child labor in factory or sweatshop. And even the men themselves suffer through overlong hours of toil. Though agriculture is not one of the most exhausting forms of labor, it is monotonous, save for the turn of the seasons, and it is often solitary. Even its advanced forms often confine the solitary workman to the ceaseless round of tasks in the barn throughout the day and the week. For in many cases the new equipment and the specialized lines were adopted with regard paid to the output alone, and not to the effect upon the agent.

The conditions of toil are often unnecessarily hard. Labor-saving devices in the home are sometimes scantily provided, while those for barn and field are ample. " Evil is wrought by want of thought as well as want of heart." Let us glance at a single illustration—the supply of water in the house. The Agricultural Survey of 1910 found that in Prince Edward Island ninety-seven per cent. of the farm houses obtain water from wells outside the house. All carry the water by hand. In Nova Scotia only two per cent. of the farm houses have water piped to the house. In New Brunswick ninety-five per cent. obtain water from wells and springs. In English-speaking Quebec ninety-two per cent. carry water by hand. These conditions are general. This lack is due perhaps chiefly to the fact that the equipment introduced so liberally out-of-doors is not regarded as labor-saving by the man who has no dread of toil, but rather as a means of adding to the efficiency of his labor and thus multiplying his output. But the wife suffers nevertheless, and the daughters leave. The household science courses offered by the agricultural colleges point the way to a solution. With wider knowledge of the possibilities of achievement through fuller equipment the daughters of the farm will vie with their brothers in advance.

Conditions of toil in the fields also are unnecessarily

hard. The modern crusade against occupational disease must deliver the farmer from rheumatism and many another affliction by recalling him from the fields in rain and giving him more mastery over all the circumstances of his toil. The modern world can easily afford such relief through a fairer distribution of the profits of labor.

The problem of the farm laborer is an unsolved one in Canada as yet, nor will it be solved until greater efficiency is demanded, higher wages paid, and a home for the farm laborer and his household provided. A somewhat common custom at present is to pay a certain monthly wage—the average for eastern Canada is $32.66 per month for a season of some seven or eight months—together with board at the farmer's table and a room in his house, and also stabling and keep for the hired man's horse. I recently asked one of our leading farmers regarding the effect upon the efficiency and general character of the men of this custom of maintaining a driving horse. " They are out driving until midnight," was his reply; " the effect upon both morals and efficiency is bad. But," he added, " you can secure them upon no other terms." The cottage for a home would benefit employer and employee alike. What modern industry has discovered modern agriculture must learn, namely, that the best paid and cared for labor is the most profitable.

The boarding of the hired men is often a hardship to the housewife. The custom may have national compensations. When a man of foreign nationality is hired, nothing else so effectively shapes him into a Canadian citizen. But it has personal penalties. If several men are employed the strain upon the home life is severe. I have already instanced in another connec-

9

tion a young Spencerville farmer whose father by the purchase of several farms had replaced thirty-eight persons by eight. Recently this young man told me of the decision to rent the farm, giving as the chief reason that his mother and sister were practically attendants upon the hired men. The home, which has everything desirable that country life can afford, is maintained, but the barns and fields are in the hands of renters; and the city claims another of that type which gives us nation-builders.

The result of conditions of labor on the farm is that there is little of that joy and pride in one's work which is essential to all true living. Our people need not only to sing with our poet Anderson of to-day:

> There is no land like our land,
> The sea calls to the sea;
> The mother that hath borne us
> Hath a daughter fair as she.
>
> O this may love the kopje,
> And that the blue-gum tree,
> But this land is our land,
> And Canada for me!*

but to sing in the spirit of our poet Sangster, writing just before our modern day began:

> A song, a song for the good old flail
> That our fathers used before us;
> A song for the flail, and the faces hale
> Of the queenly dames that bore us!
>   We are old Nature's peers,
>   His royal cavaliers;
> Knights of the plough! For no Golden Fleece we sail;
> We're princes in our own right,— our sceptre is the flail!†

* R. S. G. Anderson, in "The Westminster."
† Charles Sangster, Cantata, "The Happy Harvesters."

THE HIRED MAN IN THE HOME.

UNNECESSARY TOIL—WATER FROM THE WELL.
Woman's needless tasks.

The country is lacking in social life. This lack is seen not merely in what is often called society, but in its very elements. The fewness of women in the country brings severe social strain. Domestic help for farm homes cannot be obtained. In times of illness a trained nurse can be secured. During the recovery of strength neighbors render what assistance they can, but not even the services of a washerwoman can be had for hire. In May last I conducted the funeral of a wife and mother. The household consisted, in addition, of the husband and two sons under twenty. For six months a trained nurse had been in charge, but the husband and the sons had perforce to become the housekeepers. Since the funeral they have lived alone, bereaved indeed. They are well-to-do. They are eminently respectable. Yet attempts to secure a housekeeper have been in vain.

The financial relation between farmers and their children has caused many a tragedy. I could cite an instance of a man of thirty-five, married, with happy children, an elder in his church, serving upon a rich farm, without a dollar to own or to control except with the express consent of his father. The son, but not the father, holds the respect and the affection of the community. A form of trial which has made this one man strong through discipline has made countless hundreds fail. Scant appreciation, little relaxation, and lack of financial provision annually drives many promising youths from the country to the city. Financial equality between husband and wife; wise rewards to the child for mastering tasks, leading on to a definite understanding over independent responsibility, are called for.

Means of social life, in the ordinary acceptance of that term, are lacking in the country. A questionnaire sent out to a number of my acquaintances brings more evidence of this than of any other lack.   One woman quotes, in passionate protest, the words of Cowper:

> O Solitude, where are the charms
> Which sages have seen in thy face?
> Better dwell in the midst of alarms
> Than reign in this desolate place.

The hunger for comradeship drives many a migrant from the country to the never-filled cities.   This need must itself be met, for though there are compensations in the country, " to speak of them is scarcely more effective than to reason with the avalanche concerning the glory of the mountain after it has felt the joy of yielding to the forces that have pulled at its heart since the world began."*

The social life of pioneer days had two characteristics absent from that of the present.   The essential operations of the farm brought people together.   Logging was perforce a common task.   There was not capital in the hands of the pioneers to secure its performance by paid labor.   The nature of the task did not permit of its being done single-handed.   And so it was with many other operations as well.   The " bee "—the word does not arise from the social habits of the honey bee; word and institution alike came down from ancient Saxon days, when an alarm of danger from a foe brought all together for defence—the " bee " to which men had recourse for mutual aid in labor availed for social utility as well.   And the other characteristic was that the satisfaction of ends attained gave place for

* Wilbert L. Anderson, " The Country Town," p. 196.

social purposes. Men felt that they were gaining what they lived for, and so when some weeks of comparative leisure came at different seasons of the year, a household would go to spend the greater part of a happy day with another household in social enjoyment. Neither of these sources of social activities is found with us at present. The newer and better agriculture is richer by far in potentialities of social satisfaction through collaboration than was the earlier primitive form. But these potentialities are not yet being taken advantage of as they might and should be. The use of machines made it possible for men to labor more alone. The advance in modes of agriculture has opened men's eyes to a vision of things to be achieved, but attainment has not come, and every moment and every energy are devoted to the progress or the prosperity so ardently desired, while the needs of the social life are forgotten in eager pursuit of the material goal.

Yet there are instances everywhere to be found foreshadowing the coming good. I have mentioned a gathering of seventeen farmers on silo-filling day, none of whom used tobacco. Yet the group to which they belong has maintained a Pipe-club, and jolly good times have been enjoyed at its meetings. They are remodelling their barns, employing modern adaptations of cement and improved water systems. For the installation of these improvements co-operatively they formed a Pipe-and-Wrench Club. An annual business meeting was necessary, and of the first a social function as well was made, with wives and daughters present, and after-dinner toasts. The meetings of the club then became monthly affairs, with papers read, discussions, and music. It is along some such lines as these that a better social life on the farm must be built up. The new social satisfactions must be linked with the new economic co-operation.

The rural telephone is having almost revolutionary effects in answering social need. There is a local telephone company for Augusta and Edwardsburg townships, with central exchange in Spencerville, whose capital is provided solely by our farmers, and whose board of directors is composed of farmers. It has already placed telephones in over five hundred homes, and is rapidly extending. And again this is to be noted: the social benefit arises through an instrumentality introduced not for our social but for business purposes. In this it is typical of all real betterment. Rural mail delivery is also affording help, although upon intellectual rather than upon social lines. From the village of Spencerville five delivery routes radiate, serving approximately four hundred homes. Another local institution of a genuinely social character is the agricultural fair. The township one held in Spencerville is the year's chief visiting day for hundreds of households. And again we notice that this instrumentality has been maintained in social efficiency by remaining true to its agricultural character. Those fairs in neighboring towns which commercialized their attractions, depending upon hired entertainment for drawing power, are dying or dead; this and similar ones depending upon interest in farm products and handicrafts are growing in patronage.

The country is lacking in healthful recreation. Play is almost unattainable in country schools under present conditions. We have many hundreds of schools with an attendance too small to secure efficiency along any line.

servers that one reason why farmers co-operate so little
is that they have not learned team-work through play
in youth. Play is one of the most ethical of all human
activities. In other activities we are largely controlled
from without. In play we are most free. Play is
spontaneous, and therefore self-expressive, and thus
ethical. But it has also another great meaning. It is
in play that the instinctive aversion of one individual
to another is most fully overcome, and the social spirit
is fostered. It is when individuals come together with
pleasure that they merge so as to become a society, a
community.

An unsolved problem is as to how the recreations of
country life may be so associated with its tasks that
boys and girls shall regard farm life as a desirable
vocation. The recreations of the country must become
native and significant; must have a true relation to
real life in the country—they cannot be exotic. The
farmer distrusts the city reformer's knowledge of rural
life, and humorously depicts it:

> I would flee from the city's rule and law,
> From its form and fashion cut loose,
> And go where the strawberry stands on its straw,
> And the gooseberry grows on its goose.
> Oh, let me drink from a moss-grown pump
> That was hewn from a pumpkin tree;
> Eat mush and milk from a rural stump—
> (From form and fashion free);
> —New-gathered mush from the mushroom vine,
> And milk from a milk-weed sweet,
> With luscious pine-apple from the pine—
> (Such food as the gods might eat),
> —And then to the whitewashed dairy I'd turn,
> Where the dairy maid hastening hies,

Her ruddy and golden butter to churn
From the milk of her butter-flies;
And I'll rise at morn with the early bird,
To the fragrant farm-yard pass,
As the farmer turns his beautiful herd
Of grasshoppers out to grass.

Yet he accepts his recreation from town. With much better cause might he discount amusements of the Coney Island type proffered him from the city than flout its well-meant social guidance.

The country is lacking in means of education adapted to country life. Here we touch upon one of the most direct and active causes of loss of rural population. Those boys and girls who take fullest advantage of the public school go on to the high school, business college or university, and almost invariably enter teaching or other of the professions or business life. A two-fold injury is wrought by our present educational system. Not only are some led directly from the farm. Others, seeing no connection between their studies and life, lose all interest in study, and take up the tasks of the farm unprepared to appreciate what is best in farm life. Every child is entitled to an education that is at once cultural and vocational. A vocational course lays the foundation for technical or professional skill and efficiency; it should also show the pupil how to use his vocation as a means of personal growth, intellectual and moral, and how to make his vocation a means of service to his fellow-men. There is a one-roomed public school within my congregation, at Ventnor, where for the past three years there has been a school garden with experimental plots cultivated by the pupils. Last year the chief kinds of fodder plants were the subject of ex-

SCHOOLHOUSE IN EDWARDSBURG, ONTARIO.

A school with enrolment of one.

periment. With what zest those plots were cared for! The study was intended to be vocational, but there was no subject taught in that school more cultural; not only so, but every cultural subject benefited by the presence of the one vocational one. Pupils, learning for real life, became eager for all education. Again, when I first knew Spencerville few of the school children could name the wild flowers; some could not even recognize the forest trees. The school principal had the boys begin a collection of native woods. It aroused such interest that a collection so excellent was secured that when once the Governor-General visited the Brockville schools to grace the opening of the Macdonald Manual Training School, the loan of this collection was asked for by the county superintendent as an exhibit. Now, this study of native woods was taken up as cultural. It gave some boys at least such a new interest in the country that it proved vocational as well, fitting them for, and retaining them upon, the farm.

Not only is the chief trend of our present mode of education away from the farm, but as compared with the same mode of education in the cities our country schools are inefficient. In the city teaching is made a life vocation; in the country it is made a stepping-stone to some other career. The average time spent by our rural teachers in this profession is less than four years. Of all city teachers professional training is demanded; in the country many are permitted to teach, not only without professional training, but even without a certificate of general attainments. Moreover, even with ill-qualified teachers, country schools are more expensive than city ones, inasmuch as adequately paid teachers for well filled classes cost less per pupil than the poorly paid teachers with one or two pupils to a class. In Manitoba during the year 1910 there were 62 districts operating schools with an enrolment of 10 or less, the total enrolment being 321, averaging 5.1 per school. These districts spent $35,707, which means that the education, such as it was, cost $111 per child, based on the average attendance. In marked contrast with these figures are those of the city of Winnipeg, where the cost per pupil was $34, and this included a full collegiate course, together with manual training and domestic science for children in the grades, and school buildings as complete as any in Canada. The era of consolidated schools must come. These will secure an abler, better qualified teaching force; equipment for carrying on work of a vocational nature; the numbers of pupils needed to carry on organized play, the grading of pupils, and an adequate school programme; and the housing and other facilities requisite for the social, recreational and cultural activities of an organized social centre.

There is a pitiful lack of appreciation of country values. One of these is the beauty of nature; the love of animals is another; the privacy and freedom of life another; environment essentially healthful and creative another. But such values are countless,—wide as human life itself and varied as its needs. Even in the new industrial life farm values stand easily first. In the factory the mechanic tends one operation of one machine; on the farm a man must master all operations of a score of machines. One becomes a machine-tender; the other an artisan and engineer.

But these values are unappreciated. Few of those who are freeborn heirs of the country are awake to the charm of the fields. A farmer may be grandly master of his business and at the same time, with Lampman, thrill with the joy of the earth:

> The broad earth bids me forth.   I rise
> With lifted brow and upward eyes,
> I bathe my spirit in blue skies,
>   And taste the springs of life.
> I feel the tumult of new birth;
> I waken with the wakening earth;
> I match the bluebird in her mirth;
>   And wild with wind and sun,
> A treasurer of immortal days,
> I roam the glorious world with praise,
> The hillsides and the wooded ways,
>   Till earth and I are one.*

Few know the birds, the common flowers, or even the forest trees, and as for the native shrubs they are quite nameless. This lack is general. An English observer writes: "There is no help in visions of Arcadia; yet it is plain fact that in days gone by the peasantry found life more than endurable. They had their folk-songs, now utterly forgotten. They had romances and fairy-lore, which their descendants could no more appreciate than an idyll of Theocritus. If your peasant love the fields which give him bread, he will not think it hard to labor in them . . . There was a time when the old English names of all our flowers were common on rustic lips—by which, indeed, they were first uttered. The fact that flowers and birds are well-nigh forgotten, together with the songs and the elves, shows how advanced is the process of rural disintegration."†

* Archibald Lampman, " Lyrics of Earth."
† " The Private Papers of Henry Ryecroft," p. 202.

It was my privilege to attend the first Students' Convention at Northfield—that gathering of college men at which the Student Volunteer Movement began. One day a few of us were off for a tramp over the hills. Coming across some huckleberry pickers we bought a few berries. As we paid a woman for them I said, "What a glorious view you have from these hills!" With mild profanity but with strong feeling she replied: "You wouldn't think so darn much of it if you had to make a living here picking blueberries." There were forces of feeling pent up within that woman's nature, but resentment only at hard conditions was felt. I have a friend, one of the largest-natured and truest-hearted of all our ministers of the Gospel, who in his youth was a gardener on one of Scotland's great estates. Flowers in garden and greenhouse were grown in utmost profusion. Seldom were they seen except by the servants who tended them. Thousands were cut daily and thrown aside. Hard by was a great industrial city, yet none of its people, destitute as they were of flowers and of all forms of beauty, were ever permitted to see one blossom of the boundless store near by. As a consequence, to one true heart which until then had loved flowers they are now a source of pain. So, with some who dwell in the country, all nature is so intimately blent with associations of toil that it cannot be looked on with pleasure. With yet more these sensibilities have never been aroused. The latent power was there, and, as the harpstring vibrates when a note is struck on a string of similar pitch, might have awaked at the touch of nature-love in another heart.

A FLOWER-LOVING FARMER, INDIAN HEAD.

HOMESTEAD GARDEN, INDIAN HEAD, SASK.
Appreciation of country values.

With beauty God covers the ground; no acre too poor to
    befriend,
That thou and I and all men may perceive and comprehend.*

But in childhood neither did parent speak of love of
beauty at home, nor did teacher impart it in school,
nor were its fountains in literature discovered.   And
as a consequence a great human need is unmet.   The
unesthetic rural mind starves amid scenes "where the
spirit of beauty dwelleth," as though seamen should
perish of thirst as they sail in the mouth of the broad
Amazon.

There is truth in Edwin Markham's arraignment
of society in his greatest poem, " The Man with the
Hoe " :

Bound by the weight of centuries, he leans
Upon his hoe and gazes on the ground;
The emptiness of ages in his face,
And on his back the burden of the world.
Who made him dead to rapture and despair?
A thing that grieves not and that never hopes,
Stolid and stunned, a brother to the ox?
Who loosened and let down that brutal jaw?
Whose was the hand that slanted back this brow?
Whose breath blew out the light within this brain?
What gulfs between him and the seraphim!
Slave of the wheel of labor, what to him
Are Plato and the swing of Pleiades?
What the long reaches of the peaks of song,
The rift of dawn, the reddening of the rose?

One perhaps resents the application of this strong por-
traiture of the peasant of Europe to any class of our
people.   One may go further and say: This is what
the intuition of the poet saw in the great painting;

    * Bliss Carman.

but what did the intuition of the artist see in the human
life there portrayed? Was it not the deathlessness of
the home affections and the sensibilities of religion?
True; yet poet and painter are alike right, and the
question for us in Canada is this: Though religion
and love be unquenchable, do we wish to retain these
sensibilities only?—to retain them on the terms of the
life Millet depicts and Markham censures? Turn we
to another great French painting, Jules Breton's
" Song of the Lark," and ask: Why should we not
retain the rapture visible on this peasant girl's face as
she listens to the morning song of the lark while
trudging barefoot to her toil, without retaining the
narrowness of her peasant life? We ask also: Though
there are many among our farmers who are far from
insensible to " the rift of dawn, the reddening of the
rose, and the long reaches of the peaks of song," aye,
and who " feel all the passion of eternity," yet why
should " time's tragedy " be in " their aching stoop "?
Why should they so bear " upon their back the burden
of the world " that " through their bent shape humanity
cries protest " ?

> Is this the thing the Lord God made, and gave
> To have dominion over sea and land?
> To trace the stars and search the heavens for power,
> To feel the passion of eternity?
> Is this the dream He dreamed who shaped the suns
> And pillared the blue firmament with light?
> —Down all the stretch of hell to its last gulf
> There is no shape more terrible than this,
> More tongued with censure of the world's blind greed,
> More filled with signs and portents for the soul,
> More fraught with menace to the universe!
> Through this dread shape the suffering ages look;

Time's tragedy is in that aching stoop;
Through this dread shape, humanity—betrayed,
Plundered, profaned, and disinherited,—
Cries protest to the judges of the world,
A protest that is also prophecy.
O Masters, Lords and Rulers in all realms,
Is this the handiwork ye give to God?
This monstrous thing, distorted and soul-quenched?
How will ye ever straighten up this shape?
Give back the upward looking and the light;
Rebuild in it the music and the dream,
Touch it again with immortality,
Make right the immemorial infamies,
Perfidious wrongs, immedicable woes?

Who, one may again ask, are the " Masters, Lords and
Rulers in all realms " who are responsible? Not only
those whose oppression brings about such woe, but also
all who might relieve that woe. Dr. Henry Sloane
Coffin, of Madison Avenue Presbyterian Church, in
his recent volume, " Social Aspects of the Cross,"
writes thus of the viewpoint of Jesus: " Again, and
this is more surprising, Jesus numbered Himself with
the transgressors. There is not the slightest indica-
tion that He felt Himself a sinner. The keenest conscience our world has known found nothing with which
to charge itself. There is no expression of penitence
and no prayer for forgiveness among the personal
prayers of Jesus. But this does not mean that He
considered Himself without responsibility for the
ignorance and folly and iniquity of the world in which
He lived. While fully aware of His uniqueness,
placing himself apart from and over against the rest
of humanity, Jesus realized His oneness with men in
all that they achieved or failed of, suffered, or enjoyed.
10

If there was a Zacchaeus whose honesty and generosity
had given way under the bad system of revenue-col-
lecting them in vogue, Jesus felt Himself implicated
in his downfall.   If there were sick folk, their diseases
were to Him, in part at least, due to inherited weakness or wrong conditions of life which might frankly
be termed devilish, but for which He felt Himself
socially accountable."

And if we, His followers, do not try to better human
living, Markham's final question concerns us:

> O Masters, Lords and Rulers in all lands,
> How will the future reckon with this man?
> How answer his brute question in that hour
> When whirlwinds of rebellion shake the world?
> How will it be with kingdoms and with kings—
> With those who shaped him to the thing he is—
> When this dumb terror shall reply to God
> After the silence of the centuries?

The country is lacking in community ideals.   What
patriotism is to a nation such ideals are to a locality.
Solidarity is one of these high ideals, the oneness in
being and in interests of all.   But in the country as it
now is there is no magnetism to touch its atoms with
the power of affinity and make them cohere.   The rural
community is but ropes of sand where it should be
chains of steel.   There are localities here and there
throughout the country where more of such solidarity
exists than is generally found.   Roebuck, the neighborhood in which is situated one of the three
congregations in my pastoral charge, has always,
through some kindly influence, retained something of
this.   The two denominations chiefly represented in the
community, Methodist and Presbyterian, are singu-

larly free from sectarian feeling. Their Sunday-school work has always been carried on as a union enterprise. Two school districts more than a generation ago built one school in common and have since had a large district school carrying on public school work in two grades, under two teachers. In other ways the people of the locality act as if integrally one. May it not be largely in consequence of this solidarity that there is found there a larger farm population than can be found elsewhere in the county of Grenville?

The church, too, is lacking in certain regards in the country. This is due not to absence of devoted service on the part of pastors and church workers, but to need of redirection. And lack here is more far-reaching in effects than at any other point. The church is, of all institutions, deepest in the affections of the greatest number of persons. If there be an unsatisfied hunger that she alone can meet, that want must touch rural life at a more vital point than any other. Let us notice such lack in two directions only. The farmer is entering a new world-environment for which the church is called upon to fit him. He no longer meets face to face those with whom he deals. He sells by sample for delivery at a distance, and must learn to deliver goods up to sample. He is entering upon new relations with his neighbors through co-operation. The greatest ethical task of each generation is to provide new forms of guidance for such new conditions as these. The greatest ethical task for the church in the city is to place within the new corporate industrial and commercial organizations the controlling motives of justice and brotherhood. The most fundamental honesty to-day deals with unearned profits. So the greatest ethical task of the church in the country is to lead the farmer to feel the new responsibilities arising out of the new agriculture so that he shall enter upon them with a new sense of personal worth and of service rendered.

And the church is called on to render social service in the country. By this we do not at all mean that she is to become institutional. That may follow incidentally. But she is to seek not simply the regeneration and the spiritual culture of individuals, but also the transformation of every relationship and every institution now conformed to the spirit of this world into the blessedness of the kingdom of God. The church is now valiantly fighting the liquor traffic; she must deliver rural society in like manner from every adverse encumbrance. And she must foster every organization and agency that strives for the enrichment and enlargement of life. An ancient philosopher defined the freeman by no contrast with the slave, but as the man who lives in a state where there is no slave. Even so there can be no happy man until no one is unhappy. The church is to serve until there is no preventable misery.

> I will not cease from mental fight,
> Nor shall my sword sleep in my hand
> Till we have built Jerusalem
> In England's green and pleasant land.
> —*William Blake, " Social Advance."*

THE FUNCTION OF THE CHURCH

"They are all living monuments of a dead church," said
Frances Willard once in speaking to Dr. Josiah Strong, of the
Red Cross and similar movements. "Nay," was the reply,
"She is not dead, but sleepeth."

Wild, wild wind, wilt thou never cease thy sighing?
　　Dark, dark night, wilt thou never wear away?
Cold, cold Church, in thy death-sleep lying,
　　Thy Lent is past, thy Passion here, but not thine Easter-day!

Peace, faint heart, though the night be spent with sighing;
　　Rest, fair corse, where thy Lord Himself hath lain;
Weep, dear Lord, where Thy bride is lying,
　　Thy tears shall wake her frozen limbs to life and health
　　　again.
　　　　　　　　　　　　　　　—*Charles Kingsley.*

　　　I pray you look over the walls of your creed,
　　　　Heaven-centred and staunch as they seem,
　　　At the manifold forms of human need
　　　　With which the ages teem.
　　　　　　　　　　　　—*Arthur Wentworth Eaton.*

CHAPTER V.

THE FUNCTION OF THE CHURCH.

The farmer is engaged in a struggle which is affecting every situation in the country and every institution. It is in this struggle that the farmer now needs religious help. Shall the church give him in this crisis theological teaching only—pure, it may be, as to its source in the Word of God, but still purely theological? Or shall she, not turning aside from this, busy herself also with all his varied interests, social, educational, recreational, and even economic? What, in meeting such a situation, is the function of the church?

In New England there has been a clashing of policy as well as of viewpoint upon this problem, between the Evangelicals and the Liberal Christians. The Liberal Movement stressed humanitarian types of uplift to such a degree as to become a sociological rather than a religious movement for betterment. The Evangelicals stressed the teaching of the Christian pulpit, depending upon its fruits in personal character; claiming that New England, cradled in theology, had produced her superb manhood in the past, with its outcome in civilization, by means of her orthodoxy. Each side had its limitation of view. Those who advocate reliance upon pure theology overlook the fact that the Pilgrim Fathers came to New England purposely to seek a new social environment, and that this new environment gave an

151

open field for the beneficent influence of theology. They overlook also the fact that in the New England of the past century, where preaching became most individualistic and unpractical, the rural exodus became most exhausting. Dr. Warren H. Wilson says: " The only areas of country life known to me in which people do not go to church at all are in New England and among colonies of New England people. . . . I think the preachers of New England who taught individualism instead of social efficiency had a hand in this."*

Those who place the stress upon pulpit teaching in its best form of strong and sane evangelism, but still with neglect of social efficiency, overlook the fact that New England was the cradle of the strongest evangelism of the past generation under Dwight L. Moody. Those who place reliance upon humanitarian efforts overlook the fact that New England has been even more markedly the home of unsuccessful social experiment than of unsuccessful religious individualism; and also that the only communities in the United States of America where the present rural problem has not arisen—the Dunkards, Mennonites, and other Dutch and German communions, and to a considerable degree the Scotch and Scotch-Irish communities—there has been found not only greater social efficiency, but also clearly defined theological discipline; while both schools alike overlook the fact that in the few but great examples of downward rural tendencies being checked and replaced by uplift of the finest character—such as, on the local scale, in the Steinthal under Oberlin, and on the national scale in Denmark under Gruntvig—are examples of the welding

* " Men and Religion Messages," Vol. VI, p. 261.

into one of spiritual culture and social service. No controversy is ever settled save by the logic of facts, and the logic of facts, through the verdict of the historical outcome, is putting an end to this controversy in New England. "What we are now getting," says Dr. George F. Wells, " in the evangelical and missionary movements of the present day, is a theology socialized— the things of faith humanly lived and taught . . . while the danger, if not the guilt, of the liberal movement, because of a too persistent emphasis, is that of not becoming a part of the socialized church she has helped to nurture, and thus of becoming ineffective as a mere sociology."*

The liberal movement claims to have taught the church that she has a social task, and the claim is admitted by many. But there was another and earlier teacher. The tasks undertaken by Christian missionaries abroad formed the first leaven; and the Salvation Army—whose revered leader, knighted long since by the sword of the Spirit in Immanuel's hand, has just been called to the presence of his great Commander†— was the effective pioneer. And without being cognizant of the details one may safely assume that through whatever group the impulse in New England came, it was neither the blind passion of outraged humanity nor the patient insistence of the scientific spirit, but the power of the Holy Spirit of God working by love in hearts renewed by faith in Christ which there as elsewhere called the church's attention to the need of fuller, wider social service.

---

* " An Answer to the New England Church Question," p. 8.

† General Booth's death had been announced in the press the day before the first delivery of this lecture.

We need not therefore ask, Is the function of the church primarily theological or primarily sociological? It is neither. Her function is religious. Now, religion is not a science, but a department of life, whereas theology and sociology are sciences. And religion, as life, has need of both sciences as her handmaids.

The devotees of sociology are fain, meanwhile, to inform us that theology fails even to define the church as a social institution; theologians are but too apt to retort that sociology is incompetent to define the church, because it has no language whereby to describe the redemptional aspect of the facts for which the church stands. Both criticisms have elements of truth, but only as each science is defective. Were sociology a truly inductive science, comprehensive in its inductions, it would find the facts of redemption in human society as clearly as any other series of facts; and were theology a truly progressive science it would find in the increasing complexity of social relations, in the new problems of social ethics, and in the development of the social conscience, a realm of Godward relations the key to which is found in the scriptural conception of the church as the social institute of the kingdom of God.

We obtain the right standpoint from which to discern the function of the church when we regard it as an institute—an established organization or society pledged to some special purpose and work—whose object is the establishment of the kingdom of God in human society.

And we obtain the requisite insight wherewith to discern the function of the church when we follow the course of the providence of God and the teaching of the Spirit of God in the trend of the age.

The coming of the kingdom of God involves a two-fold redemption. There are two entities which Christ came to save, the soul of man and—not, as Rauschenbusch puts it, the " race of man," but—the whole creation. The age and the rightful use of proof-texts is not past. Here are the proofs: " Believe on the Lord Jesus Christ and thou shalt be saved "; and " The creation itself also shall be delivered from the bondage of corruption into the liberty of the glory of the children of God."

There are two methods by which the kingdom of God enters our world: " Except a man be born from above he cannot see the kingdom of God." " And I saw the holy city, new Jerusalem, coming down out of heaven from God."

In order to set up the kingdom of God in the world of men the church seeks the salvation of the souls of men by means of a service so fundamental that it has as yet no distinctive name; and she seeks the redemption of society—of the whole creation—by means of what we to-day describe as social service. The former of these, service, namely, to the soul of man, demands a specific name, even as " a host of economic terms await translation into moral and spiritual speech."* We have called it evangelistic service, but social service also is of the essence of the gospel; we have called it spiritual service, religious service, but each of these terms covers social service as well. We fully endorse the opinion of Mrs. Browning:

> What's the best thing in the world?
> Something out of it, I think.

* Charles S. MacFarland, " Spiritual Culture and Social Service," p. 18.

But we hold that the Gospel comes not only to make men fit for heaven, but to make earth fit for men. By means of these two forms of religious service the church seeks to answer in regard to every man the two primary and perennial questions of God concerning man, " Where art thou ?" and " Where is thy brother ?" The first of these questions is answered in personal regeneration, the second in social redemption. The latter is as essential to the kingdom as the former. We must seek to bring to pass a social order which shall embody the teaching of Jesus. " His teaching about the kingdom of God has its application to the society we now know as the Christian church, but has also its application beyond the Christian church to the family, the community, the state, the brotherhood of humanity, and to whatever forms of associated life are found among men."*

The denial of this dishonors God. There is an evident parallelism between the occasion, famous in Scottish ecclesiastical history, when Erskine made his plea for foreign missions and was bidden by the Moderator to refrain, with the words, "Young man, sit down. When God wishes to save the heathen He can do it without your aid or mine," and the occasion described by the Secretary of the Federal Council of the Churches of Christ in America: " Only a little while ago I heard a strange plea from a minister whose parish is situated in a great democratic manufacturing community. His advice was that we must refrain from trying to adjust the social order. He said we must leave things to God. God would take care of it, and we must not interfere

* D. M. Ross, " The Teaching of Jesus," p. 144.

with His designs."*   Gentlemen, when such a stand is taken it is time to cry with Erskine, "Moderator, rax me that Bible," and, beginning with Christ's words in the twenty-fifth of Matthew, read afresh the will of God.

The church exists to secure for all their perfect human rights. She has therefore as her fundamental task the evangelizing of all persons, and as her culminating task the glorification of life. But an essential intermediate task emerges as the consequent of the first and the antecedent of the second, namely, the training of men for world-service. As the three dimensions of length, breadth, height, exhaust space, so these three forms of service—evangelism, spiritual culture, and human service—securing spiritual life, nurture, and vocation, complete the business of the church.

From this standpoint, then, of the church as the agency of Christ in establishing the kingdom through the salvation of men and the redemption of society, we seek to discover the function of the church in the present crisis in rural life.

But vision as well as standpoint is needed. The requisite insight can only be gained as God is seen at work in the trend of the age. When the providence of God was shattering the social fabric of the ancient Roman world the Spirit of God led Christian men to one form of service; when the feudal system of mediaeval Europe was taking form, and again when that in turn was giving way to democracy, the same Spirit led on, through the trend of the age, to other forms of service. When men lived and labored chiefly

* S. C. MacFarland, "Spiritual Culture and Social Service," p. 50.

as independent persons or households, the church was
called upon to stress faithfulness in personal relationships. The need lay there; the way was open for
nothing else. But when the unit of industry and of
living becomes the group, when commerce takes form
under the chartered company and the trust, the form
of human need has changed, and the form of service
changes with it. And the form to which God is now
leading is Social Service, that is, that form of effort
for man's betterment which seeks to uplift and trans-
form his associated and community life.

Of the trend of the age Professor Law finely says in
the excellent Guild Hand-book on Social Service:
" The Christianity of our age has so far developed and
will still further develop a social conscience, which in
the breadth of its view of social duty and its sensitive-
ness to social responsibilities, marks a fresh stage in
the divine education of mankind, and in the moulding
of human life by the leaven of the kingdom of God."
If that be an excellent statement of the starting-point
of a modern discussion of the mission of the church,
the next step could not be given in a finer way than in
the later words of Professor Law: " There is perhaps
no more living conviction among us than that, if we
wish to help men effectively, we must act on them
through all the complex influences of social environment."*

But still another, a second insight into the church's
function is given us by the trend of the age. Preventive work is emphasized, rather than restorative.
The volume of the " Men and Religion Messages " dealing with Social Service opens with this striking illustra-

* " Social Service," edited by R. W. McIntosh, pp. 8, 10.

tion: " When the United States Government faced the enterprise of digging the Panama Canal it had to set about the task of creating a new Panama through which to dig it. That region had been notoriously unhealthy, so that every tie of the Panama Railway is said to have been laid at the cost of a man's life. Before taking its engineers and thousands of laborers thither, that government had to establish adequate hospital facilities and provide a competent staff of physicians and nurses; but it was also necessary to attempt to clean up the Isthmus, to drain the towns and to do away with all standing pools where mosquitoes breed, to destroy rats and make regulations at the ports so that no others could get ashore from vessels, to erect sanitary villages in which the builders of the canal could be safely kept. The result has been one of the miracles of modern times,—the transformation of a pestilential locality into a health resort; a place where no man willingly lived, who could possibly get away from it, into a place where large hotels are successfully run for steamer-loads of tourists who come seeking rest and new vitality.

" Jesus came to create a new earth . . . "*

It has ever been the glory of the Christian Church that she has acted the part of the Good Samaritan, alleviating misery, providing charity; she has founded hospitals, asylums; she has relieved, she has rescued the victims of ignorance, poverty, wretchedness, and crime. But in her earlier days, indwelt by the Spirit of her Lord, she went forth as a purifying, reconstructive power, turning the world upside down. Nor had she at any time wholly abandoned this health-giving

* " Men and Religion Messages," Vol. II, p. 1.

mission. But in these days she is coming more fully
into her own.

This is the trend of our age. More than ever before
men are seeking knowledge and control of the causes
of conditions and events. Such mastery is the whole
spirit and trend of modern science. Such is the
" dominant note of modern philanthropy. Organized
charity is now endeavoring to seek out and to strike
effectively at the causes of dependence, the organized
forces of evil, the intolerable living conditions, which
are beyond the control of the individuals whom they
injure and whom they too often destroy. Other tasks
for other ages ; this be the glory of ours, that the social
causes of dependence shall be destroyed."* Such, too,
is the modern note in the labors of the Christian
church. She is vitally concerned with the fundamental
questions of social righteousness and industrial equity.
It was her spirit that brought into being the Red
Cross Societies, but she is addressing herself to the
abolition of war. Never shall she cease to pour wine
and oil into wounds while one half-dead traveller is
found, but her truer office is not this, nor to police
the road, but to reform the system which produces
robbers.

A simple and concrete yet pertinent example which
exemplifies at once both principles, of social rather
than individual service, and of removing causes rather
than remedying results, is found in the two successive
stages of the work for temperance, as we still style it.
First came the attempt to reform the drunkard and to
conserve the boy by means of the pledge, and next the

* Edward T. Devine, " The Dominant Note of Modern Philanthropy."

attempt to prevent the making of drunkards by means of prohibition. The first method sought, by personal service to individuals man by man, to rescue fallen men, or, as individually, to prevent men from falling. The second method sought to defend a community, and that by communal action, against the presence of temptation. Preventive, rather than rescue work, is the supreme social duty of the church.

Thus we gain the requisite insight wherewith to discern the function of the church in dealing with the rural problem. In her programme there must be no social opportunism. She is not to use palliatives. She is to deal not with symptoms but with causes of disturbance, and thus effect a radical cure.

These principles must guide in her attempts to solve the city problem as well. Social settlements are imperatively called for by the present situation, but they will not solve the problem. They deal with proximate but not with ultimate causes of distress. The agencies called for to deal with these clearly lie elsewhere. To point out what these agencies are is a light undertaking; to utilize them, labor indeed. There are two central sources of power which the church must dominate for the kingdom in order to solve the city problem, —the Directorates and the Unions. Out of these two foci of potency stream the energies that make or mar the city, and the church must claim both of them for her Master. At the annual meeting of one of the great coffee-house companies of London a few days ago a dividend of thirty-seven per cent. was declared. Amid the congratulatory speeches which followed the reading of the report the question was asked by one of the shareholders: " What do we pay our waitresses ?"

11

When that question and kindred question are asked and asked effectively in the name of Christ at all Boards of Directors the first great step shall have been taken for the solution of the city problem. And the second is like unto it in validity, urgency, and potency, namely, that men should ask in the Labor Unions: " What do we give our masters, eye-service or faithfulness ?" Not the minimum wage only but the highest wage industry can afford must be granted; but with that wage must go true-hearted service.

Across the personnel of the membership of the directorates and the unions alike runs the line of universal cleavage among men, that which separates men of the world and the servants of Christ; and through these latter the church must dominate the two nuclei of life; and then shall the city—the hope and the despair of democracy, the glory and the shame of civilization,— be won for the Kingdom. All other hostile forces must soon capitulate when these protagonists become bondservants of Christ.

Another point remains to be considered. How far is the function of the church, thus understood, institutional ? The institutional church is substitutionary. One of our Deaconesses in speaking during the "Institute Hour" at the Summer School at Geneva Park touched the very heart of the matter with regard to all institutional church work, when she said that the Deaconesses had been given a beautiful descriptive name, " Vicarious Mothers." Blessings on their gracious, vicarious service ! But better that the real mothers should also serve as mothers than that we should have vicarious mothers; better the service of

MACDONALD CONSOLIDATED SCHOOL, GUELPH, ONTARIO.

The era of the Consolidated School has come.

the mother in fact though it be imperfect, than the most perfect service of a vicarious mother.

The institutional church performs for society functions which under ideal conditions belong to other social institutions. Because the homes of the slums cannot perform their rightful functions the church undertakes some of these in place of the home. There are certain primary classes of institutions such as the home, the club, the firm, the trust, the school, the town, the nation, which among them share every duty the institutional church can undertake.

The church's function is to be monitor and guide to all these. She is commissioned to go into all the world of human relationships, and disciple all nations, all societies, all communities of men, teaching men so institutionalized to observe all things whatsoever Christ hath commanded.

We have read the Great Commission as though it said "Go, disciple all persons." Its true force is that the nation is to be discipled until as such it fulfils Christ's will, and the nation here implies all forms of community life, of which it is the chief and the type.

But, though such is her full social function under ideal circumstances, nevertheless the church began her course with institutionalism. Finding then no agency in society to which she could teach His law of charity, as now she teaches the state, she appointed the seven to perform the diaconate, the social service, of an almonary society.

Moreover, inasmuch as her views upon many forms of service are ever in advance of those of all other institutions, the church must ever be, to that extent, institutional. At every new stage of progress in human uplift the Church of Christ must have her diaconate, and maintain it until all ideals have risen to her plane.

And the conditions of the rural community to-day, in failing to provide for so many human needs that those whom God designed to dwell in the country are fleeing thence, constitute an emphatic call to the church to become institutional in regard to every unanswered rural human need, until she heal country life.

"It goes without saying that much of what we call social service ought not to be necessary. It may seem a derogation from the spiritual mission of the church to engage in the efforts to secure the justice, the efficiency, the better conditions of life and work, the wide opportunities for individual and social development which it is the desire of voluntary social agencies to bring about. But until actual provision is made by the state or other agencies for the prevention of the evils and the meeting of the needs which are helping to produce the social unrest of our day, the church must stand by the work, just as in former ages she stood by the almsgiving and the ministration to individuals which have resulted in so many functions of our present governments—hospitals, alms-houses, schools and the like. When government or other agencies shall have assumed the new obligations which new social and economic conditions are forcing on us, then the church may relinquish her share in the work and press on to some other worthy task."* Then shall the Diaconate be set free for the duties of the Apostolate, and a new stage be reached in the spiritual life of man.

* "A Social Service Programme for the Parish." The Joint Commission on Social Service of the Protestant Episcopal Church.

PUBLIC SCHOOL, VINELAND, LINCOLN COUNTY, ONTARIO.

"The school will give an education for life."

THE COUNTRY CHURCH
PROGRAMME

Sow the seed beside all waters
  North and south and east and west;
That our toiling sons and daughters
  In the harvest may be blest.
Tell the tidings of salvation
  'Mid the storms of Labrador;
Speak the word of consolation
  By the lone Pacific's shore.
Where the fisher plies his calling
  'Mid the perils of the sea;
Where the forests old are falling,
Giving place to lawn and lea.
                —*Robert Murray*, "*Book of Praise.*"

CHAPTER VI.

The Country Church Programme.

President Butterfield, in his book " The Country Church and the Rural Problem," says: " I do not happen to know of a rural church with a programme of work which constitutes a really live attack upon the essential problems of rural civilization." Daring as aviator's flight and yet more full of risk may seem any attempt even to sketch such a programme. But yet to do so is simply to endeavor to translate into the terms of the concrete case before us the general programme of Christianity, which is:

> To proclaim good news to such as are in need;
> To announce release to the prisoners of war,
> And recovery of sight to those who do not see;
> To set at liberty those whom tyranny has crushed;
> To proclaim the year of grace with the Lord.

The first desideratum for such a programme is EXECUTIVE OVERSIGHT. This problem gives the Boards of Social Service another field of operation. Our efficient Secretaries, who have accomplished so much in the way of guiding legislation on moral and social problems, so much in promoting sane and strong evangelism, so much in fighting organized vice, and are now taking up lines of work which will help solve the city problem, must also become our trained and scientific leaders in this field of social service for the uplift of country life.

An extract from the " Report of Progress for 1911," of the Federal Council of the Churches of Christ in America, puts well the place of such executive oversight: " At the meeting of the Council in Philadelphia in 1908 three notable reports were made which attracted national and international attention, the reports, namely, upon ' The Church and Industrial Relations,' ' The Church and International Relations,' and ' The Church and Home Missions.' Had the meeting in Philadelphia been merely a Convention these notable utterances would soon have lost their significance. But placed in the hands of the churches with provision for permanent executive oversight they have become the source of activities of service which, it is no exaggeration to say, are affecting the entire Christian and church life of our country."

This utterance indicates clearly the weakness, not only of conventions, but of much of the business of the church. Conferences, Synods, and Assemblies adopt recommendations and pass resolutions which express with wisdom and force well-planned courses of action. But because of no executive leadership to see to the carrying out of such resolutions, much of their force is lost.

It is but a few years since the churches began appointing their Boards and Commissions of Social Service. It was then the conviction of many that the church had entered upon a new field of achievement which would yet be found to exercise as profound a change upon society, and in its reflex action upon the church itself, as even the great work of missions was doing. That conviction is strengthened to-day as we see new vistas such as this opening before us.

The services to be rendered by such an executive would consist in the exploration of the field; the planning of appropriate means of service; the holding of conferences for the arousing and guiding of opinion; and the preparation of necessary helps for the task. Yet must the church cease to look for the prophet of a wonder-working movement that shall solve our problem, and gird herself for a serious task. The need for both oversight and local endeavor is well put in the opening words of a Manual issued recently by the Joint Commission on Social Service of the Protestant Episcopal Church in the United States. " This pamphlet is the first of a series on various phases and methods of social service. It is intended to follow this initial pamphlet with others on such topics as ' The Agricultural Community and its Problems.' . . . The success of social service depends ultimately upon the efforts of the individual parish. Unless the minister of the individual church and his workers, men and women, take a hand in actual community service, the efforts of larger units, diocesan or national social service organizations, must go largely for naught. In fact a chief object of these larger bodies should be to interest the individual parish and its minister in the world-wide movement to improve conditions of life and work for men, women and children."* Such initiative and oversight an effective programme would lay upon our Secretaries of the Board of Social Service.

The next desideratum for the programme is a Survey of Rural Conditions under such guidance. In order

* " A Social Service Manual for the Parish."

to effective service the church must first envisage her task. The first duty of the physician is diagnosis. Remedies are the means by which to reach his objective —the restoration of health; but remedies are the hazard of the dice, with heavy odds against a cure, until diagnosis recognizes the disease and indicates its stage.

The church received the Survey as a means of research in her field of service, from Charity Organization. The great surveys so far, among many lesser ones, have been Booth's monumental work, " The Life and Labors of the People of London," and the " Pittsburg Survey." The Survey is an attempt to base the church's policy upon all pertinent facts. The modern world has been made the modern world by the use of just such inductive methods. This method it was with which the Dominion Conservation Commission began its work, in a survey of agricultural conditions on a thousand farms throughout Canada. It is at once the scientific method of the use of objective material, and the recognition of the organic character of social facts. The recent report of the Federal Council deals with this method under the striking caption " Standard Research and Christian Progress."

The survey is necessary because facts are elusive and illusive, hidden away until sought, and deceptive as they thrust themselves upon impression. We do not know accurately the needs of the rural community. And it is necessary also because the kind and number of human needs is not what they recently were. The values of living have changed. There are new forms of waste of human resources, and new standards of human efficiency. And while the facts everywhere have a class resemblance, they vary in detail from place to place.

" Know your community " must become the church's watchword in social service in country as in city. If it be profitable for husbandry to have experts testing and suggesting methods, may it not be more needful to have efficiency studies of rural social and religious life?

The churches adopting this agency acknowledge in doing so their past remissness. A recent typical utterance runs: " The Board of Home Missions of the Presbyterian Church in the United States of America has been ministering to country parishes for more than a century. It has sought farmers through forests and across deserts. It has built innumerable little white churches on the country crossroads for him to worship in. It has baptized his children, taught them, married them, and buried them. It has striven to save his soul—striven earnestly and valiantly, sometimes heroically. But never until within this year has it made a thorough, official and scientific study of the country community it has attempted to serve. It has done everything in its power to pave the farmer's road to the celestial city, but it has paid little attention to examining his road to the nearest village church. It has given great sums to alleviate poverty, but given little thought to the causes that make for poverty—the American system of farm tenantry, the robbing of soil of its fertility and stripping the hillside of its trees. It has pictured the beauty of the heavenly mansions and taken no account of the buildings in which men and women must spend their lives here and now. It has been a faithful steward in caring for the Elysian fields, but it has allowed the riches of blue-grass and corn and wheat-field to be squandered with prodigal hand. It has made a glorious and untiring fight to teach the chil-

dren God's word in the Bible, but it has left God's
word in the rivers and hills, the grass and the trees,
without prophet, witness, or defender.   Hereafter it is
going to know something about the communities it
attempts to serve—of what stuff they are made, what are
their needs and their aspirations.   It will take an interest in the everyday affairs of the farmer—his crops and
stock, his buildings and machinery, his roads and school,
his lodge and recreation.   The spires of the little cross-
roads church will still point to the skies, but its footstone
will lie on the commonplace work of the day.   It will
' preach the worth of the native earth,' and it will
look upon American land as holy land to be guarded
as a sacred trust from the Almighty to His children."[*]

This method is coming largely into use, as an instru-
ment by the churches.   During last year the Department of Church and Country Life of the Presbyterian
Church in the United States carried on seven rural
surveys   in   as   many   communities   and   States.
The scope of the inquiry was as follows: " Beginning
with the locality, the economic conditions as expressed
in land-ownership, wages, labor conditions, and the
' money-crops ' of the district, and proceeding through
an analysis of the population, of the social mind, means
of communication, class distinctions, social organizations, the investigator approached last of all the in-
quiries as to moral conditions and religious institutions,
and the final inquiry had to do with the social welfare,
conceived as a resultant of the various processes under
study."[†]

In 1909 a survey was carried on jointly by the Fed-

[*] " A Rural Survey in Missouri," p. 3.
[†] " A Rural Survey in Pennsylvania," p. 3.

eral Council and the Home Missions Council.   Its purpose was to discover the amount of " overlapping " in
mission work.   It revealed instead so great an amount
of " overlooking " of need that those who were supposed
to know most about conditions almost resented the findings.   But this survey has become the historic seed of
nation-wide activities.   One of its fruits was the decision, in January of the present year, of the Home
Missions Council, consisting of representatives of the
boards of home missions of the twenty-four leading
denominations in the United States, to carry out, as a
common undertaking, a survey of every State from
Kansas to the coast, in order that " the endeavor to
Christianize a continent be based upon the widest possible basis of ascertainable facts."*

Material is abundant for use in the direction of such
a survey.   George Frederick Wells has published an
excellent manual, " A Social Survey for Rural Communities."   The Commission on Social Service of the
Protestant Episcopal Church has issued another, entitled " A Social Service Programme for the Parish ";
the Young People's Missionary Movement, a third; the
Russell Sage Foundation a more comprehensive one for
general use in city or country.   " The method is correct, and it is the only corrective method."

One of the needs revealed by every survey yet made
gives us the next desideratum for the church's programme, Church Union, or, where organic union be not
feasible, Federation.   The situation shows the absolute
necessity of co-ordinating our forces.   Not the planting
of the church in immigration areas alone, but the orien-

* " Consultations upon Western Neglected Fields," Home
Mission Council, p. 3.

tation of the church to her task throughout the country, calls for the setting free of efficiency unencumbered by the brakes of denominational rivalry. In communities where different denominations became established half a century ago, where commodious church buildings were erected forty years ago, designed to accommodate larger congregations than then existed, where depletion of population commenced thirty years ago and has already carried off one-third of the population for which those churches were built, as imperative a situation is found as any demanding co-operation in the home mission field.

And the logic of the situation points to organic union. There appears no practical reason why the Presbyterian Church in Canada and the Presbyterian Church in the United States should unite organically. Their duty might be to federate for the solution of similar problems. But where several churches serve one community, where their work interlaces, organic union, if possible, is the rational course. As well divide our school work sectarianly and hope to have it efficient; as well have three competing schools in each hamlet; as well have children in the open country pass by a school or two in order to attend that of their grandfather's preference, and expect a scholarly community, with education efficiently applied to life, as hope for the best results religiously in serving our farmers' homes by our divided church life.

Some fear that the absence of competition would lessen the church's activity. One of the most fruitful of modern conceptions is that of the efficiency engineer. He examines the expenditure of labor in a trade—that of the bricklayer, for instance, and points out how by different movements of the hand and trowel labor may be halved and efficiency doubled; he scrutinizes an organized business and points out where leakages occur, where poor co-ordination is found, where efficiency might be promoted.   The Dominion Government has at present an English expert investigating the working of the Departments with a view to efficient reorganization. The tests of the efficiency engineer applied to the churches would show that their efficiency lies not in the competitive spirit but in spiritual consecration.

But if organic union be not possible, co-operation as frank, as full, as free, as if denominations were organically united is imperative.   To serve our land in her need every church must work, not for the church in either its local or its connexional interests, but for the kingdom of God.

In the United States men have no hope of any speedy organic union on a large scale.   But forty denominations, forming practically almost the entire constituency of evangelical Christianity, have formed a Federal Council which is becoming the central agency in country community betterment.   The movement anticipates union.   Dr. Tallmadge Root, one of the Secretaries, says: " Conditions demand co-operation everywhere and consolidation somewhere.   The question to-day is no longer between isolation and co-operation.   The only alternative now is between temporary or permanent, spasmodic or systematic, co-operation.   Federation means co-operation systematic and permanent.   It is indispensable, not only for present efficiency, but as the first step towards church unity."   As between the denominations the plan is federated action, but as regards the local situation the outcome in " one-minister federations in country villages " is practically union. A difficulty in the administration of these has, how-

ever, arisen, through the custom of having these ad-
ministered by the authorities of the different denominations in turn.   George Frederick Wells, lately Research
Secretary of the Federal Council, a recognized authority
on the matter, says: "Transitional Federations, where
churches for a time have to relate themselves to different
denominational organizations, suffer from too much
friction." We are fortunate in possessing in Canada
a more promising agency, in the Joint Union Committee with its new function of oversight and administration, for such local union churches, awaiting the coming of the organic union to which we look forward.
Meanwhile, here, as in the United States, "the para-
mount end is the establishment of efficient co-operation
among evangelical denominations so as to meet the
unmet spiritual needs of America and bring about the
establishment of the kingdom of heaven here."

The next requisite in the programme is Special
Training for the Ministry.   Not that there should be
one class of ministers trained for the country and
another for the city.   We desiderate one civilization
in city and country alike in which all shall be at home,
and therefore reprobate any further distinction of class.
But special training is called for in methods of dealing
with this problem on the part of all ministers, so that
those whose lot happens to fall in the city shall have
a sympathetic understanding of it, while those whose
choice is the country pastorate shall have efficient equipment for their tasks.   To some slight extent, perhaps,
elective courses of study may prove necessary, though
only in a limited field.   But there is need of training
for all alike along new lines—of direct contact with
social problems under the teacher's eye,—that is, for

the use of the case-system or clinical method; and for the adoption as a main subject of research, of the study of the relation of the kingdom of God to the associative life of man.

The next requisite in the programme is the direct Ministry of Teaching upon the problem. The church must, from her throne of power, the pulpit, preach a message for the times. The need of the hour is that of a clearer understanding on the part of Christian men and women of the present situation.

We even venture to suggest some topics of discourse, not as exhaustive, but suggestive; and first the Problem itself. We as pastors need to take up with our people a serious study of the problem. Evidence accumulates from many quarters that our people will welcome such discussion. These needs are very real in the experience of our people, though inarticulate. Their very expression is itself the first step towards setting at liberty those who are crushed.

Again, we should speak upon the merits of life on the farm. There is indeed an attraction in the city:

> The sun's on the pavement
>   And the current comes and goes,
> And the grey streets of London
>   They blossom like the rose.
> The bluebells may beckon
>   The cuckoo call—and yet,
> The grey streets of London
>   I never may forget.
> And the green country meadows
>   Are fresh and fine to see;
> But the grey streets of London
>   They're all the world to me.*

* Rosamund Watson, " A Song of London."
  12

A true life may be lived anywhere:

> O Love builds on the azure sea,
>   And Love builds on the golden sand,
> And Love builds on the rose-winged cloud,
>   And sometimes Love builds on the land.
>
> O if Love builds on sparkling sea,
>   And if Love builds on golden strand,
> And if Love builds on rosy cloud,
>   To Love, these are the solid land.
>
> O Love will build his lily walls,
>   And Love his pearly roof will rear,
> On cloud or land, on mist or sea—
>   Love's solid land is everywhere!*

And yet—those expert judges in the things of the heart, the Poets, being witness—the country is peculiarly the home of the home.

> Happy the man whose life's full round
> Is passed within his farmstead's bound;
> Who in his elder years may view
> The self-same home that as a boy he knew.
> Fortune upon him has no hold
> With its alarms and tumults manifold;
> He does not flit on fickle wings
> Slaking his thirst at unfamiliar springs.
> Active still and stout of thew
> A hale old man, he lives three ages through.
> Others may seek the changes travel gives:
> They see more life, but he more truly lives.†

And even the ascetic life—when, under Bernard of Clairvaux with his Rule of Charity, it abandoned cities

---

* Isabella V. Crawford, "Malcolm's Katie."
† Claudian. Translated by George S. Bryan, "Poems of Country Life."

"LOOK HERE, UPON THIS PICTURE, AND ON THIS."

THE COUNTRY NEEDS A VISION OF ITS OWN
FELICITY.

and the sciences to render valuable service in the development of agriculture—wrote over the portals of its rural hostelries:

> Here man more purely lives, less oft doth fall,
> More promptly rises, walks with nicer heed,
> More safely rests, dies happier.*

The worth of rural life is seen more clearly still by contrast through the bare, bald recital of Frederic Harrison's tremendous indictment of modern industrial conditions in British cities: " To me at least it would be enough to condemn society as hardly an advance upon slavery or serfdom, if the permanent condition of industry were to be that which we now behold—that ninety per cent. of the actual producers of wealth have no home that they can call their own beyond the end of the week; have no bit of soil or so much as a room that belongs to them; have nothing of value of any kind except as much furniture as will go in a cart; have the precarious chance of weekly wages which barely suffice to keep them in health; are housed for the most part in places that no man thinks fit for his horse; are separated by so narrow a margin from destitution that a month of bad trade, sickness, or unexpected loss brings them face to face with hunger and pauperism.   This is the normal state of the average workman."†   Thorold Rogers, too, declares, " There is every reason to fear that it is the case that there is collected a population in our great towns that equals in amount the whole of those who lived in England six centuries ago, whose

---

* Wordsworth, " Sonnets."

† Address before Industrial Remuneration Congress, quoted in " Social Advance," by David Watson, p. 91.

condition is more destitute, whose homes are more squalid, whose means are more uncertain, whose prospects are more hopeless, than those of the peasant serfs of the middle ages or the meanest drudges of the mediaeval cities."* How different our Canadian rural life:

> City clangors are far behind us,
> Dusty streets and noisome air;
> Ruthless toil can no longer bind us,
> Liberty shatters the gyves of care.
> Green are the hills which the clouds float over,
> Mountains of pearl in a sapphire sea;
> Zephyrs are laden with scent of clover
> And rural melodies, blythe and free.
> Herds of cattle in grassy meadows
> Mottling the valleys, recline at ease—
> Ruminate dreamily under the shadows
> Cast by the graceful sheltering trees.
> Orchards laden with apples and peaches,
> Fields that are white with the waving grain,
> Bounties of nature and industry teach us
> Lessons that memory long shall retain.
> Here and there by the trees half hidden
> We catch a glimpse of a pleasant home;
> And the thought springs up to the lips unbidden,
> O why should Canada's children roam?†

And again, we should speak of the improvement possible in farm life. I am asked a question: Should the church undertake to teach agriculture? and a second one: Should the church tell men how to raise better cabbages? It was my purpose rather to emphasize the better social life. But let us consider. Until the present year this particular branch of the church main-

* Thorold Rogers, "Six Centuries of Work and Wages," p. 47.
† Edward Hartley Dewart, "Songs of Life."

tained a university. She might as legitimately maintain an agricultural college if the nation should fail to do so. The same branch of the church teaches the Bhils in India how to farm. Under stress of circumstances she might do so elsewhere.

> There are no heathen oaks, no Gentile pines,
> The soil whereon we stand is Christian soil.

Should she teach men here how to grow better cabbages? She need not. But she should teach men everywhere and always that it is their duty to grow better cabbages. Each of our Provinces provides most helpful agencies of agricultural improvement; it is for the church to deal with the moral prerequisites of better husbandry, and hold out the better resultant life as an incentive.

If husbandry, amplified by reclamation, perpetuated by conservation, fostered by science, may become all that we have seen possible when the whole wide world shall become a garden, what of the Edenic life obtainable there? " God's partner in making the new earth " is Dr. Robertson's definition of the young modern farmer, and he gives thereby a glimpse into the inexhaustible life attainable by country people, who despite every wasting force are still the wellspring of national strength.

We should remind our people that as the farmer of to-day has risen far above the status of the past, so further advance is thereby made still more possible; as machinery has already lightened toil, its further services may be yet more significant; as the telephone, mail-delivery and other agencies are now enriching rural life, other and finer facilities are practicable. We should speak of what education might do in a merely

material way for the farmer. A recent social survey
near Ithica, New York, covering a county, revealed the
fact that the annual labor income of farmers having a
high school education was $304 larger than those hav-
ing only a district school education. The high school
course was for them equivalent to an endowment, at 6
per cent., of $5,066. The annual labor income of
farmers with some agricultural college training was
larger by $588. For these the high school and college
training was equivalent to an endowment of $9,800.

We might speak of what intellectual entertainment
has done at Hesperia, Michigan, to bring satisfaction
at home, renown abroad, and to bestow world leadership.
Twenty years ago an annual school convention began to
gather farmers and teachers to discuss their problems
and entertain one another. Orators of world-wide fame
now feel honored by being asked to speak at Hesperia.
The county is sending forth from her own sons educators,
statesmen, and authors to serve their generation and
bring fame to their birthplace. We should remind
men that the defects of country life are of a kind more
readily remedied than are the defects of city life; that
the means of immediate betterment along some lines are
quite at their command; and that to flee from environment instead of improving it is to confess failure, to
be swayed by circumstances instead of ruling fate. The
country needs a vision of its own felicity.

Again, we must preach that the very function of husbandry, which is to furnish man's daily bread, lays
upon men a duty. It imposes an obligation similar
to that lying upon a soldier at his post. Not upon all
persons. Of the youths growing up in a rural community one may be markedly mechanical in his tastes,

may understand mechanism at a glance, and by nature's gift move fearlessly among machinery as its conscious king.   Another may be as eminently fitted for the field of commerce; he is at home amidst the forms and calculations of business, and comprehending the laws of trade is the very wine of life to him.   Another may be as markedly musical in his tastes, and still another a lover of literature; while to another, spiritually minded, there comes the call of the Spirit to the service of Christ in His ministry.   For such the field of duty lies elsewhere.   But for the man who loves the soil, whose delight is in the care of stock, the man who though he may make his way in the city—for he is country-born and therefore strong, country-bred and therefore versatile—yet must ever look back with longing to the farm,—for him the farm is the place of duty. He is called to furnish men's daily bread.   To live in this spirit is to make husbandry a noble form of human endeavor.   Such an one need never ask the question of the discouraged:

> "What is there left for me beneath the sun?
> My labor seems so useless; all I try
> I weary of before 'tis well begun;
> I scorn to grovel, and I cannot fly."
> "Hush! hush! repining heart! There's One whose eye
> Esteems each honest thought and act and word
> Noble as poet's song or patriot's sword.
> Be true to Him: He will not pass thee by.
> He may not ask thee mid His stars to shine
> And yet He needeth thee, His work is thine."*

And this is but to say that his duty is part of a universal human duty—to serve.   We must preach that the

* John Reade, " The Prophecy of Merlin."

spirit of Christ brought into business life would give all labor alike, on farm, in factory, or at the desk, the dignity of service. Then each man, producer or trader, would take out of the product or the turn-over, not a fortune, but a livelihood, and let the rest form a contribution to human well-being, in the form of zealous labor, ample wages, or a good-value product.

The minister is expected to serve for a stipend, a living. The physician, though he charges fees, is expected to put service before remuneration; the soldier serves for a livelihood, and is expected to lay down his life at need. And all the truly great in the field of science have been too devoted to their profession to seek wealth. Our Christian business men must learn to live thus as well. We are not to ask for this service up to the measure of Christ, but in His spirit. His rule is to be ours: "I am among you as one that serveth"; but His measure: "The Son of man hath not where to lay his head," is not asked of others. We must say to men: "Take your living, generous as it may be, but make your occupation service." Any man who lives by this rule would remain in the country, at his beloved occupation; for the incentives which now call men away would be gone. This, and not conscription of the youth of a nation for some years' service in subduing nature to man—as proposed by Professor James—is the "moral equivalent of war," in calling out the qualities of manhood in a people.

Is this possible? Easily, where once the demand is steadfastly made in Jesus' name. As great things have been done through lesser motives. Honor has accomplished as much. We send and are sent as guests into chambers with fittings of silver, and never a thought of pilfering or of being pilfered crosses our minds. It is not the power of the law that restrains, and, with many, not of conscience. It is habit. And even the heathen had developed a higher morality still. Until the coming of the white man the trapper of the North cached his provisions and his pelts, and the mark of the cache was inviolate. If men can standardize honesty thus, what prevents the elevating of business to the standard of service? If patriotism in time of war can make service a stronger incentive than gain, than love of of life, what cannot the potent force of Christian faith accomplish? As certainly as legislation now forbids usury, so certainly will some form of wise restraint yet prevent the taking of more than ample livelihood out of labor's return; but should those who are free from law in the freedom of Christ need aught to bind them to such service? Now, this ideal, once present, would lead men to seek that vocation where each could render the fullest service. Were it once present there would be no rural problem.

The next essential in the programme is the utilization of the agencies already at hand for the church's use.

Foremost among these is the Home. The home is the greatest agency of human welfare. It is the place where all that upbuilds does its initial, and all that destroys its final, work. Education, industry, society, and religion alike look to the home for their material. One feature of the present situation is the disregard of the home. There is a diverse characteristic of the emigration from Britain which settled Eastern Canada and that from Eastern Canada which helps fill up the West. In the one case men sought homes, in the other fortunes. Another trait of the western migration is that many go not oblivious but regardless of the fact that they take their families from homes of comfort to live for an indefinite period deprived of satisfactory home surroundings. And a chief note of the movement from the country is the making light of responsibility towards the home, towards parents who are left to carry on the farm alone. The church should lead her sons to say:

Oh, fame may heap its measure,
   And hope its blossoms strew,
And proud ambition call us,
   And honor urge us through;
But kinsfolk, kinsfolk,
   My thought is all for you!
No strange and lovely countries
   Men venture forth to view,
No power and gifts and glory
   Are worth one heart-beat true;
And kinsfolk, kinsfolk,
   My heart is all for you!*

But the church should do more than this. "Home" is not a static conception. We have passed lately from what we regarded as a static world into what we know to be a dynamic world—from a world of assorted things into a world of advancing processes. The tasks of the home itself are changing. A book upon "The Christian Home," by Dr. John Hall, popular twenty-five years ago, does not meet the needs of to-day. Changes have taken place in two directions; functions once devolving solely upon the home have been relegated to other agencies, while the socializing of life has multi-

* "Northland Lyrics," by W. C. Roberts, Theodore Roberts, and Elizabeth Roberts MacDonald.

plied the relationships of the home. While the advance of the science of education takes both teaching and training of children more and more largely out of the hands of parents; while the home is no longer related only to church and school and business, but to guild and club and lodge and office,—the church must lead the home to stress more than ever the primary and essential functions which ever remain hers. Our advancing civilization necessitates a more prolonged training than formerly for the full responsibilities of life. A chief factor in making country-born and bred men and women the leaders in all lines of national progress has been that family life which required each one from childhood's years to take his due share in the duties of the home. This home life is in danger. It must be conserved and developed. The home must still provide in childhood occupation embodying the child's tastes, the environment's necessities, the parents' wisdom; and must also provide in youth some form of economic partnership between parent and child. This age of organization demands that our youth adjust themselves to a sense of their place in organizations and possess a sense of loyalty to institutions. My boy of seven comes from his school saying, " I'm on the committee, I must see to the programme for Friday afternoon's school concert." This has the modern ring. No such training found place in my childhood. The home also must stress loyalty to itself, and the child's sense of membership should broaden out from the home relationships to those of the neighborhood and to all the institutions of society until the youth becomes a citizen of the world in the home. Our intenser life demands more recreation, our ampler life more social provision, than did

the past. The means of recreation and of social pleasures are being commercialized as a consequence. The
church must lead the home to supply an ordered provision for social as for other needs—a provision to
include all its members, the tired mother as well as the
eager daughters. The chief responsibility for the social
life of youth rests not with the church or the school but
with the home, and the fundamental social duty of the
church is to maintain the social integrity and activity
of the home. And our age of world-wide interests
demands a fuller recognition of responsibility, of the
worth of character, of the supremacy of conscience and
the duty of service, than ever before. The home has
therefore a more emphatic call than ever to provide for
social religion and personal faith. In a word, all of
those deficiencies which make conservation, progressive
farming, co-operation, social satisfaction and community service difficult of attainment must first be grappled
with in the home. What Oberlin achieved, what Gruntvig secured, is what our modern life demands and Christ
commands—the use of the home as the first agency in
upbuilding the kingdom of heaven.

The church must avail herself of the next great
agency, the School. By this is not meant any formal
control of the one institution by the other, but that the
church should inspire the school to freely fulfil more
adequately its tasks, and inspire the people to respond
more fully to the advantages offered by the school. Our
standpoint is that of the Christian Conservation Congress, which " postulated the church as the agency and
the force that is to do the work which the twentieth century demands," and " that it is the business of the
church to face fearlessly all the new problems of our

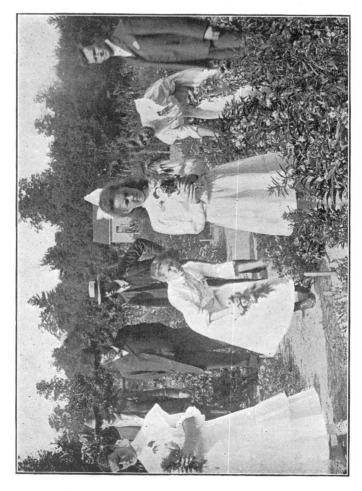

RITTENHOUSE SCHOOL GARDENS, LINCOLN COUNTY, ONTARIO.

The school fulfilling a true function.

complex day, and to grapple with them to a solution."
The whole social fabric must become a metaphrase of
the Christian life. What is needed is a body of
opinion within the church which shall understand the
school at its best, criticize it constructively, inspire it
with the leavening, uplifting, conserving influence of
religion; and shall guide the public to accept from the
school, and to ask of it, not only the intellectualizing of
the children committed to its care, but that it shall vocationalize, socialize, and moralize them as well. When,
for instance, we find in a recent report issued by the
Ontario Government the statement that "neither the
pupils nor the parents seemed to have any desire to
have agriculture taught in the school," we are face to
face with a condition in which character and motive are
the chief factors—and the church is the agency to deal
with these.

In order to solve the rural problem there is need of
widely diffused education in agriculture. The Provincial agricultural colleges cannot give this to many,
though they give it thoroughly; the coming county
agricultural high schools will be its finest agency, but
cannot give it to all. The public schools must give a
training that shall be in some degree vocational. Our
Provincial Departments of Education are offering
through the public schools elementary teaching in forestry, agriculture, and horticulture; but in these efforts
meet with a widespread lack of moral support. To
secure this is the task of the church.

But the school must do more than vocationalize the
pupil; it must do its part in socializing and moralizing
him as well. Beyond all other classes farmers find it
difficult to organize and to co-operate for mutual good.

Even when so organized Sir Horace Plunkett finds that
the local co-operative society will sell through the central co-operative agency when prices are low, but
through other channels when prices are high,

Balking the end half won for an instant's dole.

Here again is a situation which the church both directly
and through the school must meet.   The school must
adopt supervised play as a socializing agency.   Wherever
introduced, rational, normal play has promoted physical
vigor; it has aroused mental alertness more generally
than the prospect of advantage through the possession of
knowledge had done; but its especial results have been
in the realm of character.   It has solved the problem of
discipline, it has taught self-confidence and respect for
the rights of others.   It is one of the means that lies at
the basis of the solution of the rural problem.   That
problem has two underlying economic causes: insufficient production by the farmer and exploitation of the
farmer.   Industrial efficiency on the farmer's part, to
be secured through vocational education, must meet the
first; social efficiency on his part, to be secured by such
means as this, must meet the second.   Should anyone
object that such training lays an added burden upon
the teacher, an enhanced cost upon the school, the reply
lies in the comparative amounts of the cost and of the
loss now sustained by the nation through rural depletion.   The efficiency of supervised play is recognized
by all educationists.   What is still requisite is a sense
of the urgency of the situation upon their part, and an
acceptance of their view of its efficiency by the public.
To inspire educationists and public with this sense of
urgency and efficiency is the task of the church.

The Consolidated School, that has proved such an educational advance in Ohio and Indiana and is spreading so rapidly throughout the United States, has been a pedagogical success in Canada, but, so far as its wide adoption is concerned, a practical failure. In Manitoba and in New Brunswick, however, the movement is making good progress. People are getting for their children, through more primitive methods, as good an education as they desire for them. But the principle of the consolidation of schools has undoubtedly made good in meeting country needs. It is for the church to help in securing the working of that principle.

If the church undertakes her part in inspiration and moral support the outlook is bright indeed. Here is the voice of the Province of Ontario in official utterance: " The country school of the future will be teaching agriculture. It will not be a new kind of school simply because it has added a new subject to its list of studies. But in the teaching of this new subject it will find a new service in the community and a new meaning for education for country people.

" It will be the local experimental farm in a simple, but effective way; it will introduce new varieties of field crops and test methods of cultivation through the children's school-farm; it will be the local beauty-spot, with neat fences, well-kept buildings, lawns, and flower beds; it will be the local play-ground, not only for the children, but for the grown-ups; it will be the local centre for social gatherings; its library will serve everyone with books, magazines, bulletins and reports that concern themselves with the farm work in home and field as well as with literary matters.

" In the school work it will not consider examinations

as the be-all and end-all of its effort; it will not cheat the many for the sake of preparing a few for advanced work in a higher school; it will remember that most of the pupils will have only a short time at school and a long time at work, and it will make its instruction fit the needs of the worker no less than the future needs of the scholar; it will try to keep the boy who is not clever in book-studies at school and to educate him through practical activities with tools and in the garden; it will remember that children are educated for life through activities in play, in work at home, in handling tools, in experiences in Nature's Workshop, no less than by learning from books; it will bring the fathers and mothers back to school again by using the daily home interests as the means of education of their children.   It will give to our boys and girls in the country an education for life."*

But better still, here again is the official voice of that efficient Department in direct recognition of God as the goal of its labors:

I teach
The earth and soil
To them that toil,
The hill and fen
To common men
    That live just here;

The plants that grow,
The winds that blow,
The streams that run
In rain and sun
    Throughout the year;

* Ontario Department of Education. Circular No. 3, 1912.

RITTENHOUSE SCHOOL, LINCOLN COUNTY, ONTARIO.

An instance of wise philanthropy.

And then I lead
Thro' wood and mead,
Thro' mould and sod
Out unto God;
With love and cheer
I teach!*

Education in the city owes much to the gifts of philanthropy; in the country, as yet, little or nothing. To
ask from men of wealth recognition of rural needs is
not to pauperize the country; to claim equality of treatment with the city is no more than to demand simple
justice. Buildings, equipment, endowment, are lavished
upon the city by men who indeed made their fortunes
there, but made them by means of sturdy country
strength, used, often, in controlling sources of affluence
whose origin is in the country. Such men owe the debts
of philanthropy to rural rather than to urban need. An
instance of a wise and generous gift for better education
in the country is found in the Rittenhouse School in
Lincoln County, Ontario. Mr. M. F. Rittenhouse having won ample means in lumbering, acknowledged the
debt he owed to the old one-roomed stone schoolhouse at
Jordan Harbor, where he had received his education, by
giving to the neighborhood a well-equipped modern
school. Two school districts were united. The philanthropist in the case presented the enlarged district with
a graded school equipped for manual training and
domestic science, having a school garden and ample
grounds furnished with facilities for supervised recreation. The school grounds are four acres in extent. Not
yet satisfied with this provision for the neighborhood,
the donor went farther. Across the highway from the

* L. H. Bailey, quoted in circular cited.
13

school was a finely-wooded knoll of five acres. As this could not be secured separately he purchased the farm of which it formed a part. In the grove he had built a hall for community purposes, with large lecture room, library, museum, and all facilities for a social centre. The hall with its five acres of grounds he presented to the school district; the remainder of the farm to the Provincial Department of Agriculture for a demonstration farm for fruit-growing. The highway passing the school he had rebuilt on the finest lines for some two miles, having it boulevarded and provided with bridges of artistic beauty. An impetus has been given to the whole neighborhood. Land in the vicinity has trebled in value. The adjoining school sections have been stimulated to similar activities. Mr. Rittenhouse's action is an example which should call to the front many philanthropists.

The church should avail herself in the country of an interdenominational agency which has been found of great service in the city—the Young Men's Christian Association. Had it not been for this institution social need in the city—so far as the church's ministry thereto is concerned—would have been as scantily supplied as in the country. The average city church does nothing more for those beyond its membership, and scarcely more for those within, than does the country congregation, in all that pertains to the physical and recreational, and the social life. The Association, however, has done a magnificent work for young manhood through its gymnasiums, its athletic clubs, its recreation-rooms, its social parlors, and its classrooms. It has not only rendered direct service but has stimulated

MACDOUGALL HALL AND ST. PAUL'S CHURCH, ORMSTOWN, QUE.

A rural church social centre.

other agencies to greater activity, and has leavened all athletic and recreational life with a nobler spirit. All that the city has received through the Association the country requires and deserves. We have already three County Associations in Ontario—in Bruce, Huron and Lambton. Fourfold activities are carried on, physical, social, educational, and religious. The finest achievement of the Association is in developing leadership. The secretary is the pastor's strongest reinforcement. The Young Women's Christian Association offers itself as a similar agency among girls and young women. That organization lately approached the Federal Council of the Churches in the United States with this request: " The Young Women's Christian Association, in its newly developed rural work, has been grateful to recognize its entire allegiance to the church, from which it draws its inspiration, and whose work it constantly seeks to advance. . . . We should be especially glad, therefore, if the Federal Council could make it plain to the churches that the Young Women's Christian Association is an arm of the church, and that it stands ready to do work for them whenever they need help in specialized work for the women in a community."

A denominational and congregational agency to be availed of is the Men's Brotherhood. Within the congregation this organization is fitted to perform the service which the Association renders for the county. The Brotherhood seems especially adapted to meet the present situation. It is an organization of men. It is at once intensely spiritual and thoroughly practical in aim. The manliness of Christ is its inspiration; His sympathy with men its pattern. Its avowed first object is to lead men into fellowship with Christ and His church; its second, to seek the welfare of men in their relations with each other and with the world as a place for all men to live; and its third to give all men, especially in times of need, the help of Christian comradeship. Other church agencies adapted to such services are the Young People's Guild and the Christian Endeavor Society.

The Young Men's and Women's Christian Associations are fitted to supply permanently the needs of the marginal classes in the country as in the city along recreative and educational lines; brotherhoods and guilds to supply permanently within the congregation similar needs. But a direct and immediate duty lies before the church to fulfil another temporary social want institutionally. She needs to avail herself, for the present crisis, of a new agency, the social centre. In my native village of Ormstown, Quebec, is a building bearing my family name, MacDougall Hall, built as a memorial to a beloved uncle, a farmer, by his brother, another farmer, and presented to the Presbyterian Church in Ormstown as a home for the social activities of the church—the first of its kind in Canada. The donor was in advance of his time in providing such a social centre. Moreover, in his presentation of the hall to the church, he expressed the wish that the trustees should hold the building not for that congregation's use alone, but for any social activities the sister denominations might wish to engage in; not only so, but that the building should be open for any community gatherings also. Macdonald College opened its recent Provincial campaign of " Taking the Agricultural College to the Farmer " in MacDougall Hall.

Other institutions, notably the school, are being called on to provide centres for social life, and are doing so. In many parts of the United States legislative sanction has been given for the use of school grounds and buildings for such purposes when not required for class work. The meetings so held are not solely nor chiefly for sociability, but for untrammeled discussion of community problems and a purposeful programme of activities. But so far as used for purely social gatherings they lay an additional duty upon the church. It has been found that where schools were thrown open without provision for guidance in such social work, where it was supposed that attractive social surroundings without supervision would make for character-building, such gatherings became a blot on the community rather than a help. Even more imperatively than does recreation, social centres require supervision. This would seem a task too delicate and too responsible for our public school teachers, immature as they so often are. The call is for leadership in numbers sufficient and in strength adequate to supply a distinctively character-building atmosphere. In other words, this widespread movement in regard to the schools is but an additional call to the church to provide social centres.

In this form of service, as in others, material equipment is no panacea. The Spokane Chamber of Commerce in a recent utterance calls for a Country Life Hall in every community in the State. But the real leaders in the rural life movement are emphasizing leadership as the prime necessity and manifest diminishing concern over fullness of equipment.

Beyond that of adopting new agencies of service another duty lies upon the church. The modification of the primary occupations by modern industrial development, which is the real cause of the present rural problem, demands study and action from many institutions. Educational, industrial, recreative, fraternal, political organizations have functions, responsibilities and duties to undertake in regard to this problem. The church, while she is to fill these organizations with spiritual men, to inspire them with a spiritual character and a Christian ideal, must also recognize the supremacy of each in its own domain, and the necessity of the contribution of each to the solution of the problem. Thus, recognizing the unity of the problem and the solidarity of the forces which unitedly must solve it, she is called upon to assist in the federation, "upon the level" of all forces of progress.

Moreover, the Christian Church must awake to the fact that she has a competitor for the suffrages and the domain of the rural community in one of the most astute of selfish agencies—Mormonism. While not disdaining to dominate the city this system seeks first the sceptre of the open country. Its dream is of world-conquest. It behooves the church to match against the iron unity of Mormon discipline the living unity of her faith, against the inducement of a sensual life the incentive of a consecrated one, and now, before it be grown strong, to free Canada from this incubus.

Such a programme calls for self-denial and devoted service on the part of the church, but it leads to victory. "Are we, the churchmen of this continent, prepared to undertake any such programme as the regeneration of society until all social institutions attain the measure

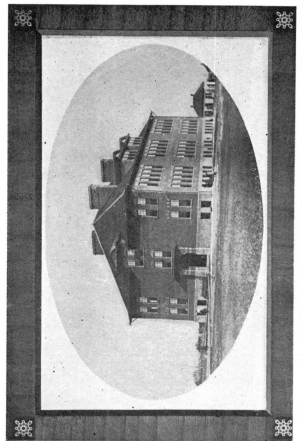

MORMON SCHOOL, TAYLOR STAKE, RAYMOND, ALBERTA.
A competitor for the sceptre of the country.

of the stature of the fullness of Christ? Are we prepared as families, as business firms, as labor organizations, as cities, as a nation, to make the venture of the Son of Man when He set His face steadfastly to go up to Jerusalem, and stake everything on love? . . . Through many tribulations we must enter into the kingdom of God. ' It became Him, for whom are all things, and to whom are all things, in bringing many sons to glory, to make the author of their salvation perfect through suffering.' The households, the corporations, the unions, the municipalities, the nations who would lead many of their brethren into the glory of the kingdom of justice, kindness and faithfulness, and be the author under God of their social salvation, cannot expect a different perfecting of their Messianic vocation.

" But the cross for Christians can never be more than an incident. ' Christ Jesus died, or rather is risen to life again, who is also at the right hand of God.' We cannot anticipate a destiny less exalted for any family, or firm, or organization, or country, which dares to make the experiment of incarnating in its life the spirit of Calvary. And there is no other way of placing a home, an industry, a settlement, a state, at the right hand of God."*

> From ocean unto ocean
> Our land shall own Thee Lord,
> And filled with true devotion
> Obey Thy sovereign word.

* " Men and Religion Messages," " Social Service," p. 117.

Our prairies and our mountains,
  Forest and fertile field,
Our rivers, lakes and fountains,
  To Thee shall tribute yield,
Till all the tribes and races
  That dwell in this fair land
Adorned with Christian graces
  Within Thy courts shall stand.

            —*Robert Murray, "Book of Praise."*

STUDENTS AND THE RURAL
PROBLEM

From life's enchantments,
  Desire of place,
From lust of getting,
  Turn thou away and set thy face
    Toward the wilderness.

With awful judgment,
  The law, the rod,
With soft allurements
  And comfortable words, will God
    Pass o'er the wilderness.

The bitter waters
  Are healed and sweet;
The ample heavens
  Pour angels' bread about thy feet,
    Throughout the wilderness.

The tents of Jacob
  As valleys spread,
As goodly cedars
  Or fair lign aloes, white and red,
    Shall share thy wilderness.

And Carmel's glory
  Thou thoughtest gone,
And Sharon's roses,
  The excellency of Lebanon,
    Delight thy wilderness!

—*Anna Bunston.*

CHAPTER VII.

Students and the Rural Problem.

I count myself happy,—in coming, at the close of our study of this problem, to an aspect of more personal interest,—in that I address a company of students. " Tell me what the young men of Oxford are thinking," some one has said, " and you will tell me what all England will be saying presently." This is said not by way of flattery, but of help. I bring you not honey but a spur. And of all students, one is happy, when speaking of social service, in addressing students for the ministry. You remember the famous picture, " The Lion's Cubs." A group of boys from one of the great schools of England stand before Nelson's monument in Westminster Abbey. One can read the look of high resolve upon their eager faces as they gaze at the figure of their hero. He is England's lion; they his cubs. Valor lives and glows again in them through his great life. Of the young warriors of the Messianic King the Psalmist declares: " Thy people offer themselves willingly in the day of thy power: in the beauties of holiness, from the womb of the morning, thou hast the dew of thy youth." The glow of consecration to service is upon the faces of the Lion of Judah's whelps as they contemplate the life of service of Jesus of Nazareth.

In considering the relation of students for the ministry to the problem of the country church, let us notice, first, that students to-day have the spirit of social service. I speak not yet of them as the college has moulded them, but of the student class as they are to-day in themselves. Back of the college lies the social preparation, undirected of human purpose, in the environment of the boy life. This spirit may not as yet be articulate, but it is apt to be there. For our students come from homes in touch with the movements of to-day. If from farm homes, as so many of them are, then from the homes of those farmers who are farming well. Their fathers and brothers in all probability have had some contact with the forces that are making for scientific farming, if not through attendance at the agricultural college, at least through familiar use of its bulletins. They are not from the homes of farmers who are failures, those growing antiquated, those becoming decadent. If from the industrial ranks, then from homes which are in touch with the forward movements of the great labor world. It was ever so. But, someone may say, Do not students often come from the homes of the poor? Granted; but in what wise poor? From the homes of widows of fine extraction, from the homes of the poor who aspire; not from the sinking poor or the degenerate. They are sons of the morning, men of the coming day.

Environment as well as origin gives them the spirit of the present, the social spirit. The youths growing up in the homes of our Canadian churches are fed upon the bread of social service. The church papers, *East and West,* for example, and those of the other denominations in equal measure, present it most attractively. The pages of all Sabbath-school publications teem with it. In our fine and strong religious fiction, such as

Ralph Connor's and Marion Keith's works—though even to mention these is injustice to those passed by—social service is ever the background on which the plot is laid. And when we touch the highest levels of literature of the past quarter-century, the " long reaches of the peaks of song," in poems such as " The White Man's Burden " and " The Man with the Hoe," social service is ever their theme and inspiration, their burden and their fire. And again it was ever so. Our English literature begins with " The Vision of Piers Plowman," —a vision of social good, one which anticipates in a marvellous way our modern needs and methods—nor has there ever been lacking in that literature, from the day of Langland's hot invective to the day of Kingsley's clarion note, the signature which Frederick Harrison in his " Studies of Victorian Literature " finds at its very heart: " Literature to-day has many characteristics, but its central note is the influence of Sociology." Under such influence our students receive the groundwork of the social spirit on which to build. Conscience, with them, is apt to be awake to social responsibility.

But we turn aside to notice as to our second point that the regulations under which our college courses are planned do not call for the teaching of social science as fully as they might. The Rev. Charles Stelzle, Secretary of the Department of Church and Labor of the Presbyterian Church in the United States, last year addressed a letter to each of the 184 theological seminaries in the United States, asking these questions:

" Please state what practical social service experience students receive while in the seminary.

" Do you have a course in social teaching?

" What is the total number of hours devoted to all

lectures during the year, and how many of these hours are given to the study of social problems?

"Is any attempt made to acquaint the student at first hand with social problems either in the city or in the country?

"Would you introduce more sociological study if you had the necessary money?

"Have your students asked for additional courses in sociological subjects in the seminary?

"Is the student offered special inducements in the form of scholarships, for example, in order that he may take additional sociological work?

"What is your general opinion of the value of sociological training for the theological student?"

Of the 184, replies were received from 80. Now, in drawing an inference from this slight response we must recognize that Mr. Stelzle is an outstanding man, a recognized leader. He has the approval of the National Government of his country for services rendered as a mediator in labor disputes. His questions in a field which he has made his own should therefore have been looked upon as of serious moment. They should not have been looked on as an impertinence. And doubtless they were not. We can only infer that failure to respond was confession of lack and of consciousness of lack. In these 104 seminaries there is doubtless no training whatever in social service.

Of the eighty from which replies were received about two-thirds were offering some kind of sociological course. But with most of them this meant only the study of the Mission Sunday School, the Rescue Mission, hospital work, and similar philanthropic and religious enterprises. Should we apply a similar test to the medical colleges, asks Mr. Stelzle, and find them limiting their students to the study of medical agencies, and making no provision for the courses in hygiene, diagnosis, or clinical practice, what should be the verdict we would give?

Of these 80 seminaries, not more than one dozen had anything like an adequate course in the matter of sociology. Even of these Mr. Stelzle makes this criticism: They handicap the study of social problems by offering incentives to follow other courses. Yet practically every seminary responding was convinced of the value of sociological training for the theological student, although there were some notable exceptions.

Thus we come to our third general head, that there is an imperative call, based not upon such opinion, but upon fact, which opinion follows slowly, for courses in the teaching of sociology in our universities—in case of their failure, in our colleges—and for courses of training in social service in our colleges. For we live in a recently made world. Down to the dawn of the nineteenth century the work of the world was done by muscular power. Each man was independent in his use of this power. Then came steam with more efficient power. But its efficiency varied with the scale upon which it was utilized. Therefore men concentrated for its utilization. This brought interdependence instead of independence among men. Men are massed and organized as never before. And that is the new civilization.

But we live also in a still more recently made world of service. In 1910 the Russell Sage Foundation published the results of an investigation of the social movements organized on a national scale in the United

States. Their number as tabulated is in the neighborhood of seventy. The order of their appearance, and
especially their rapid increase with each decade, is
instructive. The six decades before 1880 gave rise to
13; the decade of the eighties to 4; of the nineties to
12; the opening decade of this century to 39. Earliest
among those named—the earlier associations for the
reform of the drunkard are not included—came an
association for the care of the insane, then one for the
prevention of illiteracy; the American Association for
the Instruction of the Blind followed after an interval;
and then, rapidly, the American Prison Association,
the Public Health Association, the Women's Christian
Temperance Union, the Purity Alliance, the Association for the Feeble-Minded, and the National Conference on Charities and Correction. The eighties gave
rise to the Red Cross Association and the Christian Social Union. The nineties brought social
settlements, women's councils, the National Council of Mothers, the Anti-Saloon League, and movements for regulation of industries and of immigration.
After 1900 came a host of movements for the prevention of child labor, of infant mortality, of blindness,
of tuberculosis; for the education of backward children, of negroes, the care of delinquents, of epileptics;
for the suppression of the white slave traffic, and prevention of infant mortality. The various denominations organize for social service—the Presbyterian
Church's Department of Church and Labor; of Church
and Country Life; the Methodist Federation for Social
Service; the Industrial Committee of the National
Council of Congregational Churches, the Social Service
Commission of the Protestant Episcopal Church, the

Commission in Social Service of the Federal Council of the Churches of Christ in America. The social movements in the American Republic thus tabulated by the Sage Foundation have their counterpart in every line of helpfulness in all lands. Their emergence is evidence of an organic world-movement. The Church of Christ can no more resist the impulse to take part, and the leading part, in this world-movement than can the living tree in spring resist the impulse to put forth leaves and bloom and set her fruit. In these facts of the new civilization and the new impulse to service— the work respectively of the Providence and of the Spirit of God—lie the imperative call to the church, not only to labor in social service, but to take her place in teaching and in formulating the sciences which deal with societary forms and groups and with social processes.

Now our subject at this hour is not Sociology and Students for the Ministry, but The Rural Problem and Students for the Ministry. Our excursus was necessary, however, inasmuch as the right of way of sociology in these halls gives our problem its standing ground.

And, returning, we note as our next point that while our students have the groundwork of the modern social spirit on which to build, our working assumption regarding the status of the country ministry is not favorable to generous service for the solution of the rural problem. Our theory of the ministry is correct enough,—we must recover its working reality. In theory all are equal in standing; a Moderator is, by definition, but the *primus* among *pares.* In effect, we grade men according to their charges. Men should have weight according to personal worth and service

14

done, and not according to field of labor. There is one
department of our work in which this is the case—the
foreign field. We do not say Japan is a more important field than Korea, India than China, and group
men accordingly. Yet we do say city and suburban
congregations are important, the hamlet unimportant;
and rate men's standing by such criteria. Even the
efficiency of the renowned pastor whose prosperous
cause scarce keeps pace with the suburb's growth may
conceivably be less than that of the unknown pastor
whose rural charge more than holds its relative place
among the institutions of the country community. But
let us disregard altogether this equation, and note only
that the solid achievements in world-service of country-
bred men constitute an historical vindication of the
worth of rural service which renders all other vindication superfluous. We make no special plea for the
country ministry; we postulate equality in recognition
of worth in every field of service. Judged by present
standards Labrador would be rated an unimportant
field; service, and not parish, is the ground upon which
Wilfred Grenfell is appraised among the King's
laborers.

Coming now nearer the heart of our subject, we
discover that the Christian ministry in the country constitutes to-day a call to men of the best type. Even
were country life to become a by-product of civilization, successful Christian service there, judged from the
modern standpoint of the value of by-products, would
be of prime importance. Its presence or its absence
would still be the decisive factor in determining the
worth of Christianity to the world. But country life
is no mere by-product. President Butterfield, of

Amherst College, recently said: "For the next twenty years we may expect the country life movement to have great influence on the course of events. Politicians will use it as a means of riding into power. Demagogues and fakirs will take advantage of it for personal gain. Writers are even now beginning to sensationalize it. But there will also arise country men with statesmanship in them—if not, we cannot make the progress we need. The movement will have its significant national aspect, and we may look for Governors of States, and perhaps more than one President of the United States, to come out of it."

I almost feared to quote this passage, lest my purpose should be misconstrued, lest you might suppose I said: "Then you too may find position through this crusade." My purpose is simply to point out that this estimate of the movement by such a man as President Butterfield implies that an important field of service is found in the country church to-day. The country call is one to stir the blood, alike because of possibilities of failure and of achievement that lie before the country community.

Her risk of failure which may affect the world is evident. In "Who's Who in Canada" for last year 85 per cent. are country-born. Ninety per cent of our ministers of the gospel come from country homes. Henry Wallace, of *Wallace's Farmer,* Iowa's leading journalist, writes: "It is from the rural population that the cities of this land, of all lands, in all ages, have drawn the vigorous blood with which to replace the enormous waste incident to city life. It may in fact well be doubted whether cities of over 50,000 could continue to prosper, to govern themselves, or even continue in existence worth while, without this stream of fresh blood from the country, with its cool nerves, firm muscles, and good habits."* The " Law of the City," as well as the " Law of the Yukon," is given by Robert W. Service in the words:

This is the Law of the Yukon, and ever she makes it plain:
" Send not your foolish and feeble; send me your strong and
     your sane;
Strong for the red rage of battle; sane, for I harry them sore;
Send me men girt for the contest, men who are grit to the
     core;

.   .   .   .

Send me the best of your breeding, lend me your chosen ones;
Them will I take to my bosom; them will I call my sons;
Them will I gild with my treasure, them will I glut with my
     meat;
But the others—the misfits, the failures—I trample under my
     feet."†

That virile tribute is checked as soon as dissatisfaction prevails in the country; it ceases when degeneracy begins. In the unrest of the rural community lies the chief cause of the recent falling off in candidates for the ministry.

Gentlemen, Christ calls strong men to heathendom through the prospect of uplifting a pagan people. Does He not also call such men to the country through the prospect of upholding a Christian one ?

But I should be utterly unscientific if I made my chief plea the possibility of failure in supplying the church with candidates for the ministry, the city with the red blood of leadership; the failure to send forth these would be only symptomatic of disease in the rural

   * " Men and Religion Messages," Vol. VI, p. 119.
   † Robert W. Service, " The Spell of the Yukon."

community itself.   Here is a class larger in numbers than any other, professional or mercantile or industrial, larger than all other classes taken together; a class engaged in the most necessary of all callings—that of providing the people's daily bread; a class more dependent upon itself alone for all the possibilities of attainment and satisfaction in life than is any other class. This class is in danger of failing to provide itself with leaders through whom to exert its influence in the control of national affairs, to say nothing of guidance in local matters; in danger of viewing its own calling with disdain and fleeing from its environment in disgust. The chief call, along this line of risk of failure, is a call to uphold the finest Christian civilization in the country for the rural community's own sake.

Flowers of Thy heart, O God, are they.*

And shall they who stand, a wall of fire, around their much-loved land fail, and you take not heed? Shall they cease to march in the van in physical vigor, in material advance, in intellectual power, in social progress, in moral strength, or in spiritual life, and no clarion call be heard therein by the very strongest men who enter the ministry?

But the call for the best comes still more definitely through possibilities of achievement. In the city you may minister to a limited number of the leaders of to-day. In the country you may call forth the empire-builders and founders of the kingdom of many to-morrows. And in the country itself great events are at hand. The Country Life Movement itself calls for you. It is evident that our agricultural colleges and

* Ebenezer Elliott, Hymn, " God Save the People."

many other agencies have begun a crusade for a better rural economy. Modern progress helps it forward with the rural telephone and mail delivery; the Dominion and Provincial Governments are seeking means of fostering it; the educational forces are contributing richly; even the railway companies are sending out their Better Farming Specials. The moments of the movement are agricultural science, vocational education, farmers' co-operation, supervised recreation, community organization. That crusade needs the Christian Church at its very heart if it is to be spared the blight of materialism. Frederick Almy, Secretary of the Charity Organization Society of America, says: "The social gospel is being preached from every sort of pulpit, the stage, the pages of the novel, the magazine; until it is a wonder that the public will stand so much of it. There are signs of a reaction, and I fear for the future unless social work becomes less utilitarian. It is attacking those old enemies of mankind, ignorance and disease, with such sledge-hammer blows that they are weakening visibly. But its agencies are too material, and social work needs unspeakably the inspiration and the interpretation of its message which the church alone can give. . . . Its success depends upon whether it can get itself adopted by the church in every hamlet and cross-roads. . . . If through this alliance the modern social movement with its gospel of adequate opportunity sweeps the country, it will mean such an uplift for neglected humanity as will go far toward social reconstruction."

Gentlemen, there is in that a proffered alliance, a task in leadership to stir the pulses of the best. And if the movement beckons, still more does its outcome. That I shall not attempt to outline, but leave to your own prophetic souls. It was worth while for strong men to lay the foundations of Japan's, China's, India's uplift; it is worth strong men's while to enter this field to-day.

Do you consider that I am decrying the city pastorate —making a plea which, if heeded, would close the way for the most devoted and the ablest to enter there? Such is far from my intention. There is a call, and a great one, which is directly to the city pastorate. But if it be a love of ease or of gain or of fame which urges any of you to cast eyes of longing toward the city, you are debtors of your immortal souls to resist such a wish, and to seek a field somewhere, anywhere where such desires for fancied ease or gain or fame shall be crucified. Otherwise you shall win indeed your world, but verily lose your life.

But if there be a passion within you of brotherliness for the factory operative, and if there be reason for you to think that you can help the men of the labor unions to dominate those unions for Christ and His kingdom; or if you know yourself of the kindred of the men of commerce and of capital—if you have in you that which will make their life with its temptations and victories an open book to you—if your passionate longing be to guide these strong men to dominate the directorate boards for Christ and His kingdom, even though pitiless Mammon crush you as you succeed, then your call is to the city's turmoil and the city's crown.

Our next point is that in order to exert any continuing influence upon the course of rural development a man must become a real part of that country life. We need a permanent rural pastorate—not abiding in our charge, but in the country. In point of fact the country ministry is just at the pass where the country community stands—eager to escape to the town.   Before the ministry can correct this state of affairs in general country life, the same tendencies must be corrected in the ministry itself.

The Christian Conservation Congress held in New York in April last went about its work in the same effective way as the Edinburgh Missionary Conference of a few years ago—by the appointment in advance of commissions to study and report upon each phase of the subject.   One of these commissions dealt with the rural church.   Among its findings is the following: " We need a permanent country pastorate.   We can hardly expect that every man who takes a country charge shall remain there all his life.   .   .   .   Many strong men who succeed in country parishes will inevitably be called to city parishes.   Nevertheless, there should be developed a rural clergy as a professional group that tends to specialize itself and that tends to induce other men to make this their life work.   The idea of the country pastorate as a distinct vocation should be promulgated among young men.   The need and feasibility of such permanent service should become a part of the common thinking and talking about the country church."*

For we live in an age of specialization.   Not only so, but specialization is one of the chief of the forces which have made this progressive, successful age.   And there is place for specialization in the ministry as in any other profession.   There are indeed deprivations involved in country life, but they must be looked upon from the

* "Men and Religion Messages," Vol. VI, p. 77.

same viewpoint as those on the foreign mission field. The work itself is the foremost consideration.

If you make such a life choice, gentlemen, you will be but walking in the footsteps of noble exemplars. Oberlin declined a chaplaincy in the proudest regiment of France to become pastor of Ban de la Roche, nor could even the request of the Academy of France induce him to leave his country parsonage. Of George Herbert, who united in one person the saintliest character, the richest culture, the ripest scholarship, the finest genius, and the noblest blood of the England of his day, it was said, " He himself became a country minister that he might show how that sphere could become a field fit for intelligent, energetic, and stately living." Charles Kingsley, a brilliant and versatile genius—he was senior optime in mathematics and won first-rank honors in classics at Cambridge—at the age of twenty-two became curate of Eversley, a country parish where scarcely one person could read or write, and, though poet and novelist, popular lecturer and university professor, canon of Westminster Abbey, and chaplain to Queen Victoria, there he ministered throughout his life.   It was said in the hearing of an American bishop that the time would come when it would be as great an honor to be a successful country minister as to be a city minister.   He replied that the time was already here. and had been since Charles Kingsley put Eversley on the map of the world.   There are places whose names are yet unknown to fame.

It follows, as our next point, that there should be fuller attention given to preparation for the special tasks of the country ministry.   I have no slightest suggestion to offer here as to how this College, which has such a splendid record in preparing men for the ministry, should order its work.   Nor do I suggest that you should divide yourselves into two classes, burning the bridges between, for city and country service.   But with those of you who look forward to the country ministry, your chosen work should bear the same relation to your preparation that foreign mission work does to the foreign mission volunteer.   These men seek the full advantage of the common training provided for all who enter the ministry; their fellows participate with them in acquiring a general familiarity with the problems of the mission field; but in addition the mission volunteers avail themselves of every means of special knowledge and fitness.   They study comparative religion with the zest not of curiosity but of need; ethnic psychology has to them not an academic but a practical interest.   Moreover they form their mission-bands, their study-classes; they hold conventions, they invite addresses by specialists.   All that concerns missions they seek to make their own.   They put enthusiasm into their preparation.

For the best work in the country ministry to-day you need to become as skilled as the schools can make you in the principles of sociology, in knowledge of the industrial order, in the agencies of social service, as well as in the problems of the rural community.   And these should have for you the absorbing interest that missionary principles and practice have for the foreign mission volunteer.   Even census tables might captivate you as maps did William Carey.

Your work will call for knowledge of the sciences that deal with rural well-being, especially agricultural economics and rural sociology.   It is not enough that your youth may have been spent in the country.   One does not know forestry because he roamed the woods in childhood with delight.   A knowledge of the rural social status—of depletion, for example—is not instinctively acquired.   Residence in the country does not make one an adept in the social psychology of rural life, in isolation and its results, for example.   " How can even rural teachers learn to appreciate the social function of the rural school, except they be taught ?"

Your work calls for knowledge of the forces which make or mar country life.   You need to know the country's needs, to recognize the less patent as well as the apparent ones.   What, for instance, is lacking that so many of our country boys take so little interest in school studies ?   What are the successive unmet needs indicated in these verses:

Poor wee Sandy, he wanted to play,
But the bairns on the village green warned him away,
For Sandy was always more ragged than they—
    Fearful wee, tearful wee Sandy!

Poor boy Sandy, alack and alas!
At school he was always the dunce of the class;
" That thick-headed laddie no standard could pass "—
    Cowering, glowering Sandy.

Poor lad Sandy, he never could learn
Any business by which he a living might earn;
And the world with her weak ones is angry and stern—
    Wondering, blundering Sandy.*

What would play have done to brighten, brightness to educate, education to employ, unhelped Sandy?

And you need to know the country's wealth.   Say

* Anonymous, in " Social Advance," by David Watson, p. 252.

what one will, the country can never compete with the city in the things of the city. The sparkling, flashing, dazzling brilliance of her vivid, radiant streets by night is all the city's own:

> Give to me, Love, our London town,
> Now, when the hovering night comes down,
>   What if away there still be day,
> Naked sky over silver reaches,
> Bronze of bracken and gold of beeches?
>   Give me the woven shadows brown
>   Shot with the lights of London town!
>
> Little of stars our London recks;
> Night with her fiery garland decks
>   Light upon light as pearls strung white;
> Fast through the shadows and moony blazes
> Topaz and ruby whirl in blazes,
>   Flash in the sinister veil, the crown
>   Royal and fierce, of London town.*

And better things than those pulsing waves of throbbing light which have such attraction for many, are hers. But it is for you who are to serve humanity in the country to learn the country's wealth in the things of the country—things that the city cannot have. If the city is given a crown royal and fierce by her mechanism of light, the country's dower is the sunrise and sunset, dawn and day and the stars of night. If in the city topaz and ruby whirl in blazes, in the country is the light ineffable of all precious gems from the crimson flame of the ruby in the sunset up through the orange of the jacinth in the tints of autumn and the golden sheen of the topaz in the harvest, the living

* Margaret L. Woods, "The Gondola of London."

green of the emerald fields, the vivid azure of the sapphire heavens, to the royal purple and the ethereal violet of the amethyst as they glow in the shadow of the hills and gleam in the cloud. The whiteness of pure light, too, is hers alone, milky iridiscence as of the opal in the morning mist, " chalcedony's dim whiteness, pure-serene " in fields flooded with moonlight, lustre of pearl in the dew, the radiance of the diamond lavished on the landscape of snow. Now, the country's richness of aesthetic loveliness is but a type of her wealth for human living which it is yours to lead all men to see.

Out of the heart of the city, begotten
  Of the labor of men and their manifold hands,
Where souls that were sprung from the earth in her morning,
No longer regard—nor remember—her warning,
  Whose hearts in the furnace of care have forgotten
    Forever the scent and the lure of her lands;

  Out of the heart of the usurer's hold,
    From the horrible crush of the strong man's feet,
Out of the shadow where pity is dying,
Out of the clamor where beauty is lying
  Dead in the depths of the struggle for gold;
    Out of the din and the glare of the street;

  Into the arms of our mother we come,
    Our broad, strong mother, the innocent earth,
Mother of all things beautiful, blameless,
Mother of hopes that her strength makes tameless,
  Where the voices of grief and of battle are dumb,
    And the whole world laughs in the light of her mirth.*

And you need to know the agencies that are making for betterment. Let me mention in this connection one

* Archibald Lampman, " Freedom."

or two lines of preparation which you would do well to follow in addition to your studies within these halls. They will suggest others. First, acquaint yourself fully and practically with the work of the Young Men's Christian Association, not only as carried on among college men, but also in the range of its city activities. All that the city owes to the Association the country has a right to receive. Nor is this little. The athletic clubs, the gymnasium, the recreation rooms, the class-rooms, reading-rooms and parlors, for men and for boys, of the " Y. M. C. A." have been the chief source of supply—through the church's agency—of the needs unmet in the country. Save as represented by the City Association, the average town congregation has had but little to distinguish her from her rural sister in social equipment. Now, familiarity with its working in the city is the prerequisite for your employment of this agency in the country.

Secondly, familiarize yourselves with the working of the agricultural college. Young men aspiring to influence in journalism now regard a course in scientific agriculture as one of the important vestibules to their life work. Not a full course in such a college is called for, for you need not be technically trained agriculturists—but first-hand acquaintance with the scope of the work these schools are carrying on, and with the spirit in which it is being done. I do not ask you to accept my summing up of that work—it might appear the vision of an enthusiast. Let me rather present a sketch drawn by a practical Boer farmer on the veldt, Mr. J. A. Neser, presiding at the Dry Farming Congress of South Africa, held recently: " We have assembled to discuss dry farming, but dry farming is merely part of a larger whole—the New Agriculture. What, then, is this new Agriculture? It deals with all those things which affect the daily life of the farmer. It brings the railway to his door; demands refrigerator cars for his perishable products; forms co-operative societies for the purchase of seed, machinery, and manures. It analyzes his soil, tests his milk, builds butter and bacon factories; grades his crops, establishes land-banks and parcel posts, and erects rural telephones. It teaches him to control disease, and to grow and harvest every crop. It sends his son to the agricultural college and his daughter to the school of domestic science." In the country ministry, gentlemen, you need acquaintance with the technical side of such a movement, and mastery of its social aspect.

What is the life for which you are fitting yourselves? There are certain needs of the city which the social settlement is designed to serve. There are human needs of other kinds belonging to a class of persons very different in character in the country, to which the manse might be made to bear the same relation as the settlement does to our foreigners in the city. What is the conception embodied in the very word " parish "? Is it not just this idea of a settlement? The parish is the little world " around the dwelling," the world which the minister and his home are there to serve.

Permit me to say, in closing, that such a ministry would imply an intimate following of Christ, and must begin as His began. Being in the form of God He thought it not a thing to be clung to that He should be on an equality with God. I need recount no further step of His, if this first one you take—counting nothing that is rightfully yours of place or power a thing to be clung to. In willing consecration you are to enter on your life work.

This, again, implies prayer. It was my privilege to be at the Conference at Northfield at which the Student Movement for Missions had its origin. Men were first deeply moved at a meeting addressed by ten young men, some sons of missionaries, some natives, representing ten missionary lands. At that historic meeting, when D. L. Moody called for one speaker, Robert Wilder, to speak for India, there was no response. Neither on platform nor floor was he to be found. When sought in the waiting-room behind the platform he was discovered there upon his knees, oblivious of the passage of time. The movement thus cradled in prayer evoked a similar spirit of prayer for guidance from the great body of students present. For the next fortnight men were to be seen in groups in the rooms, and out alone upon the hills, in prayer, until Mr. Moody said he had witnessed nothing approaching it in power during his life. In order that this problem of the country church may be solved men must give themselves to the ministry for the country in that same spirit of prayer.

But those who know best how to read aright the signs of the times are clearly of opinion—the literature of service that is springing strong and full from the heart of the church to-day being their best evidence— that the Church of Christ is ready to go forward, it may be to her Gethsemane, but certainly to her glory.

> I know of a land that is tinged with shame,
>   Of hearts that faint and tire;
> And I know of a name, a name, a name
>   Can set that land on fire.
> Its sound is a brand, its letters flame,
> Yea, I know of a name, a name, a name,
>   Will set this land on fire.

RURAL UPLIFT ELSEWHERE

In some great day
  The country church
  Will find its voice
And it will say:

"I stand in the fields
Where the wide earth yields
  Her bounties of fruit and of grain;
Where the furrows turn
Till the plowshares burn
  As they circle again, again;
Where the workers pray
With their tools all day,
  In sunshine and shadow and rain.

"And I bid them tell
Of the crops they sell,
  And speak of the work they have done;
I speed every man
In his hope and plan,
  And follow his day with the sun;
And grasses and trees,
The birds and the bees
  I know and I feel every one.

"And out of it all
As the seasons fall
  I build my great temple alway;
I point to the skies
But my footstone lies
  In commonplace work of the day;
For I preach the worth
Of the native earth—
  To love and to work is to pray."

              —*L. H. Bailey.*

CHAPTER VIII.

One of the instructive historical instances of successful grappling with the problem is found in the work of John Frederick Oberlin in the Ban de la Roche, in Alsace.

True, in this case the chief factor in the present situation, the farmer entering into the industrial world, was lacking; yet the principles employed by Oberlin apply to-day. A man of genius, with a thorough and comprehensive education, of good birth and standing, he was led through deep religious consecration to accept the pastorate of Waldersbach in the Ban de la Roche, declining a chaplaincy in a French regiment to do so. The parish was a small one of about one hundred families; the people spoke a patois which could be the means of no external information; they were without means of education, and were sunk in poverty. There were no bridges whereby communication could be carried on with the outside world, but stepping-stones only over the rivers. Here Oberlin spent his life, dying beloved by his people, honored by his country and the world. He saw that to succeed in religious work he must build up the community in every way; and combining affectionate diligence in the pastorate with spiritual preaching, he added to these resolute and wise endeavor to promote education and prosperity. He began with the school and followed up with economic betterment. Having been a

227

student of engineering he summoned his parishioners to roadmaking. The land, poorly cultivated, yielded less than was needed for food for its own inhabitants. Oberlin taught better methods of agriculture,—the use of compost, the rotation of crops; he instituted an agricultural society and a school of agriculture—one of the first known—himself experimenting and teaching. He founded infant schools—the first of which history speaks—with " conductrices " to bring children to and from their homes—the Greek " pedagogue " revived. He introduced scientific methods into the ordinary schools, and instituted a higher school. The children were taught to sew, plait, and knit from earliest years; weaving and dyeing with the plants of the country were taught later. He took boys into Strasburg and had them taught trades, of which they in turn became teachers in the parish. Thus home industries were introduced into every household. The population, 500 when Oberlin began his ministry, had increased to 3,000 before his death, and this growth in numbers was the least part of the progress. The Royal Agricultural Society of Paris sent a commission to study his methods of husbandry, invited him to a more public sphere of labor, and conferred on him a gold medal. This man of genius had by his direct outlook upon life and its needs in the spirit of Christ anticipated modern education, agriculture and sociology. He had given his people the most scientific husbandry and the most advanced education known in his age, and thus secured for them economic prosperity, social welfare, and numerical growth.

In Denmark we have an example on the national scale and at the present time of the uplift of an agricultural people; and here again the impulse is due to a Christian pastor, Bishop Gruntvig,—poet, historian, patriot, educator, statesman and philanthropist.

Denmark was greatly weakened at the end of the Napoleonic wars. She was financially bankrupt, and economically prostrated by her war with Prussia, ending with the Treaty of Vienna in 1864. Gruntvig realized that if his people were to be helped the impulse must reach the mass of the people, must be linked with their daily life, and that its source must be in religion. Gruntvig's sympathies were democratic to a radical degree. A friend of the writer's was once a guest in a home in Edinburgh. A disciple of Gruntvig—a lady who had become known as a social worker in Denmark —came to the same home as a guest. At once on being presented to her hosts she asked permission to meet the maids of the house and form their acquaintance. Such is the democratic spirit of the movement inaugurated by Bishop Gruntvig. Before 1864 he had begun a " Folk High School." He sought to extend this means of education, under the Queen's patronage, as a means of rural uplift. The schools, however, extended as private enterprises. There are now over eighty of them in the country. They are boarding-schools, owned privately though receiving grants from the nation. They are permeated by a Christian atmosphere, but without formal religious teaching. There is an intense spirit of application in them, but examinations are unknown. The object sought is mental and spiritual quickening. Instruction is given by means of lectures, and is upon historical, literary and scientific subjects. Music, singing, and gymnastics have a large place. The age of admission is eighteen. Young men attend for a five months' term,—November to April; young women for a three months' term,—May to August. Fully two-thirds of Denmark's rural youth pass through them. Many attend for but a single term. To observers it is marvellous that so much could be accomplished by so short a residence. The impulse, however, is vital. So potent has been their influence that a majority of the present Cabinet Ministers of Denmark have passed through their course. The Premier has been a teacher and director in them. There are also Government high schools and agricultural schools thoroughly equipped and manned, drawing their inspiration and ideal from these Folk Schools.

Bishop Gruntvig used patriotism as one of his agencies, writing upon national history, editing and teaching the national songs and literature with such success that a cult sprang up which in over-zeal tabooed all foreign books, until a reaction set in to avoid isolation from the stream of world-literature. Meanwhile patriotism was intensely aroused. Why should not we in Canada make more of our literature?

> Sing me a song of the great Dominion,
>   Soul-felt words for a patriot's ear!
> Ring out boldly the well-turned measure,
>   Voicing your notes that a world may hear!
> Here is no starveling, heaven-forsaken,
>   Shrinking aside where the nations throng;
> Proud as the proudest moves she among them,
>   Well is she worthy a noble song!
> Sing me the joy of her fertile prairies
>   League upon league of the golden grain,
> Comfort, housed in the smiling homestead,
>   Plenty, throned on the lumbering wain!*

* Robert Reid, in Rand's " Treasury of Canadian Verse."

The graduates of Gruntvig's Folk Schools originated and promoted the many and varied co-operative societies which cover practically everything connected with rural Denmark's welfare. There are co-operative societies of production, *e.g.,* cattle breeders' associations, " control " societies for the registration of milk-yield, butter-fat, and relation of feeds to yield; co-operative societies for the manufacture of country products into finished market commodities, — creameries, cheese-factories, bacon-curing houses; co-operative societies for the storage and sale of the commodities, for the promotion of saving, and for the upholding of credit. The outcome of a passionate sense of common adversity into which religion with education as her handmaid came with uplifting power, has been a devoted, successful community service.

Co-operation began in 1882, in dairying first, then in the bacon industry, then in egg-production. The economic results soon became evident. In the next six years the exports of eggs doubled, of cheese trebled, of eggs quadrupled, and of bacon quintupled. The export of butter is now over eight-fold what it was in 1881, of eggs over twelve-fold, and of bacon fourteen-fold.* At the meeting of the British Association for the Advancement of Science held in Winnipeg in 1909 a Danish commissioner described methods by which the average yearly yield of butter from Danish cows had risen from 80 pounds in 1864 to 220 pounds in 1908. The fertility of her soil, naturally low, has increased remarkably, so that she has now the largest yield of wheat per acre in

* Monographs of International Institute of Agriculture, Vol. I, p. 159.

the world, a yield which is moreover almost double the world's average. In 1911 her average was 30 quintals to the hectare, while Britain's was 21.9, Canada's 14, that of the United States 8.4, and the average of the 22 wheat-producing countries on the five continents, 15.3 quintals to the hectare of land.* Denmark exports to other countries nine dollars worth of farm products for every acre under cultivation, although she supports a population of 155 to the square mile. The average net profit on her farms is $15 to the acre.

She has attained these results in a distinctively modern manner, by assimilating the management of agriculture to that of the great industries of the times. Most of the products are so specialized as to demand much labor, a large proportion of it highly skilled; the margin of net earnings is narrow; competition requires marketing to be of the most skilful kind. Co-operation was the sole means by which such problems could be solved. Moreover, in accomplishing these economic results, she has maintained and improved the social status. Sixty per cent. of her population is rural. Nine out of every ten of her farmers own the land they till. The average 100-acre farm employs three hired men the year round. Emigration, once large, has almost ceased—in the three years from 1905 to 1908 it fell from 8,051 to 4,558. The home life of the people has improved in every way. Sanitation, home conveniences, neatness and beauty have been secured; the love of gymnastics, of song—the rural songs of field labor, of the woods, the brooks, the birds, the love of literature, have become prevalent. The church, formerly a State institution,

* Monographs on Agricultural Corporations, International Institute of Agriculture.

DANISH HOMESTEAD.

DANISH FARMYARD.
Denmark's rural welfare has been won by Christian
co-operation.

has become more free and strongly evangelical. New church buildings are being erected by Lutherans and Gruntvigians jointly as community structures. Thus, under the impulse of a true education for practical life directed by an intense evangelical spirit and securing co-operative organization on a national scale, Denmark has been reconstructed as a nation, her depleted soil replenished, her landscape made beautiful; she has been uplifted out of a great military defeat, out of debt, out of social disintegration. She has almost closed her poorhouses and abolished pauperism. From being one of the poorest of countries she has attained the largest per capita wealth of Europe. She is a land of rural homes and of altruism.

In Ireland a remarkable advance has been made under co-operation. In 1889 Mr. Plunkett, now Sir Horace Plunkett, returned to Ireland after ten years' residence in the American West. Competition from Denmark threatened the Irish dairy industry. Government aid towards land purchase by small farmers offered opportunity for a betterment movement. Mr. Plunkett advocated co-operative societies. Fifty meetings were held before the first one was formed; over two additional years' advocacy before the second. Legislation was secured—for all the United Kingdom—by the Industrial and Provident Societies Act of 1893 and the Friendly Societies Act of 1896. The Irish Agricultural Organization Society was established to promote the formation of societies; the Irish Co-operative Agency Society to co-ordinate marketing of products. Demonstrators are employed to teach scientific agriculture on the farms. The outcome is that " in a little more than twenty years, against tremendous difficulties, in an atmosphere charged with religious and political animosities, a peace-making movement based on the principle of self-help by mutual help has been built up. All creeds and parties leave their religious and political difficulties outside, and work together. More than 900 farmers' co-operative societies, with almost 100,000 members, are doing a business of about $15,000,000 a year."* Yet even in this economic betterment the need of a deeper underlying ethical uplift is felt. " There is a tendency for societies to consign butter to the Agency when prices are low and to market their butter independently when offered good prices elsewhere."†

In the United States a widespread movement for the betterment of rural life is in progress. Attention was first called to the problem from the purely material side. The census of 1880 recorded a decrease of 5,000,000 acres under cultivation in the North Atlantic States, every state sharing in the loss. The New England Abandoned Farm discussion and movement followed. State authorities became advertising agencies for forsaken farms, seeking summer residents as purchasers. The better lines since followed are thrown into relief by the very names adopted by the organizations. What was at first a Back-to-the-farm Movement has become a Rural Life Movement. Men have turned from dealing with results to dealing with causes, from palliative measures to remedial ones.

The first helpful study of the subject, from the religious standpoint and in a constructive way, was made by Dr. Washington Gladden, who in a small volume,

* Sir Horace Plunkett, in *Youth's Companion*, Boston.

† Monographs on Agricultural Corporations, International Institute of Agriculture.

" The Christian League of Connecticut," published in 1883, gives an excellent discussion of essential principles. His larger volume, " Parish Problems," 1889, and his later one, " The Christian Pastor and the Working Church," 1898, have each chapters upon rural conditions and means of help.

The Evangelical Alliance took up the problem in 1889, when its secretary, Josiah Strong, officially " explored " five counties in the State of New York, and the Rev. Henry Fairbanks forty-four towns in Vermont. These studies included economic, moral and social conditions, population, numbers of churches, church membership and attendance. At the next International Conference called by the Alliance, in Chicago, in 1893, the problem was given a foremost place, with papers by President W. De Witt Hyde, Dr. Samuel Dyke, and others. Both of these leaders had previously written able articles on the subject, Dr. Dyke upon "The Religious Problems of the Country Town," and Dr. Hyde upon "Impending Paganism in New England." Dr. Strong's research work led to the publication in 1893 of his volume " The New Era," in which we have a clear presentation of both city and country problems as they exist and are grappled with to-day. It also led to Dr. Strong's making these and kindred questions his life work.

The American Sunday School has taken up the work of betterment energetically in wisely adopting new methods and in giving the work of the school a wider scope than before. The organized Bible Class has become a social uplift agency. Some excellent survey work has been carried on by this organization. Three years ago a prize of $1,000 was offered by the Union for the manuscript of the best essay on the problems of country communities. The prize was awarded to Charles Roads, for his excellent volume, " Rural Christendom," a work of solid worth.

The Young Men's Christian Association, which had already done so much for city life, began work for the country in 1889, when Mr. Robert Weidensall originated the " County Work." Under this plan of organization the county town becomes the headquarters of a secretary. The secretary seeks to reach every hamlet in his county and to be in touch with every congregation. The county secretary is usually an agricultural college graduate. The departments are the same as those found so necessary and successful in the city—educational, physical, social, and religious. Adaptation is sought to the needs and the opportunities of the situation. The educational work, for example, embraces farm bookkeeping, house sanitation, crop rotation. The fine work accomplished for the city along athletic and recreational lines is being wisely adapted to rural needs. The Association publishes a monthly magazine, *Rural Manhood,* dealing most helpfully with many of the problems of the rural community,—a periodical fitted to render useful service to every country minister. But the Association seeks to do more than employ its own agencies. In 1910 a country church conference was called to meet in New York by the Rural Section of the Y. M. C. A. for the purpose of securing a consensus of opinion from church leaders and other authorities on country life as to how there could best be established a basis of co-operation between the church and its supplementary agencies. A most helpful volume, " The Rural Church and Community Betterment," embodies the discussions and results. A second conference was held in December, 1911. with a similar but more constructive programme, the outcome of which is another volume, " The Country Church and Rural Welfare."

The various denominations have organized for the solution of the rural problem, and it has been found that such organization has called forth the services of some of the church's strongest men, and that the agencies thus established have quickly come to the forefront in the expressed interest of the church as well as in the manifest fruitfulness of their service. The Presbyterian Church, North, was in the van with her Department of Church and Country Work, with Dr. Warren H. Wilson as chairman. The Department has made surveys of rural conditions in Pennsylvania, Missouri, Indiana, Kentucky, Illinois, Maryland and Tennesee, of the same general nature as the great Pittsburg survey into city conditions. The results are published in most interesting documents in pamphlet form. They cover very comprehensively economic, educational, social, and religious conditions, and constitute one of those richly concrete life-studies which in this present time are laying the solid foundations of social and religious advance. But they are far from being simply studies of the situation. · Each one is an efficiency-document as well, outlining a programme of work rendered obviously necessary to the local situation. The Department of Church and Country Life has other lines of helpful work as well. During the summer of 1912 four summer schools for country ministers were carried on in widely separated territory. Leaflets and other literature are widely used, and even the picture postcard. There lies before

me a postcard stating that " The Department of Church
and Country Life advocates:

The Church as a centre for the building of the community.

The federation and co-operation of all the churches in the
community, in order to make the people one.

The consolidation of the Rural Schools for the education of
young men and women for life in the country.

The promotion of Scientific Agriculture, in order to conserve the soil for our children; to produce abundance for the
consumer; to keep the farmer's income abreast of rising
prices.

The leadership in Social Recreation for the moral development of the youth and the workingmen of the community.

Better living conditions in the interests of the future; and the
cherishing of the history of the community in memory of past
days.

Such ministry to the community that pauperism shall be
excluded and the burden of poverty lifted.

The preaching of the Gospel of Jesus Christ all the time
and in every community.

Now this postcard is itself a photograph of a poster
upon a hoarding. The moral effect of such a proclama-
tion, when lived up to, must be of the finest character.

The Federation for Social Service of the Methodist
Episcopal Church has a Commission on the Country
Church, with the Rev. G. Frederick Wells of New York
as chairman. The directness of method characteristic of
this strong denomination is shown in the action of the
General Conference in 1908 when the formation of the
Federation was approved. The Conference submitted
four questions to the Federation, asking that the findings in reply be submitted to the next General Conference: (1) What principles and measures of Social Reform are so evidently righteous and Christian as to de-

mand the specific approval of the church? (2) How can the agencies of the Methodist Episcopal Church be wisely used or altered with a view to promote the principles and measures thus approved? (3) How can we best co-operate in this behalf with other Christian denominations? (4) How can our courses of ministerial study in seminaries and conferences be modified with a view to the better preparation of our preachers for efficiency in social reform?

The Joint Commission on Social Service of the Protestant Episcopal Church is rendering efficient service with its sane and scientific work, for example, the " social service programme for a parish in an agricultural community." This church bids fair to be one of the foremost leaders in the work.

The Moravian Church, which has a rapidly expanding work in our own Northwest, recently appointed a Country Church Commission, which began its work with a thorough study of the statistics of the rural congregations for the last seven years—the first systematic effort by any denomination to separate the statistics of city and country work. The results are reported to be " of a kind that challenges the attention and calls for action."

The Reformed Presbyterian Church, whose membership is largely in the country, has, through a strong commission, of which Dr. Henry Wallace, one of America's leading agricultural editors, is chairman, attacked the problem with vigor.

Other denominations are engaged as well. The report of the Commission on the Church and Social Service to the Federal Council in December, 1912, informs us that the Department of Social Service of the

Northern Baptist Convention has taken significant action; that other denominations—the Disciples of Christ, the Society of Friends, the Christian Church, the United Presbyterian Church—are partially organized, with steady volunteer service; and that half a score of additional denominations are in process of organization in the interests of the country church and rural life.

The Federal Council of the Churches of Christ in America is becoming the central directing agency of the churches in the country life movement. This Council, formed in 1908, represents the leading Protestant denominations of the United States. It is a force to be reckoned with in every outstanding moral and social question. The Council has decided, after wide correspondence, that there is a great call for interdenominational work in the rural movement, and has under consideration far-reaching plans. Meanwhile the Council has taken various steps in co-ordinating the work. A directory of over two thousand of the organizations working at the problem has been prepared. A practical programme for the rural community has been drawn up. Information is being gathered upon what the theological seminaries, the inter-church federations, the various denominations, the home mission boards, the country life commissions, the agricultural colleges, and the philanthropic associations, are doing to promote the interests of rural life.

All of the recent strong popular movements in the churches are entering this field. The Young People's Missionary Movement is actively engaged, and has published an excellent handbook entitled " A Country Community Survey " as a guide in the investigation of conditions. The Missionary Education Movement has issued one of its textbooks upon this problem, " The Church of the Open Country," by Dr. Warren H. Wilson. The Men and Religion Movement emphasized country work. One of the seven volumes which record the great Conservation Congress deals with this subject. Book I of the volume deals with " The Rural Church of the Twentieth Century," and Book II with " Social Religion in the Country." The treatment is scientific, comprehensive and masterly.

Outside of the church's organization but in closest sympathy with it are found many promising movements. The Hesperia Movement is a fine example. In 1886 a public school teachers' association in Michigan sought added strength for its work by having the farmers meet with the teachers at their annual convention at Hesperia, a country village miles away from any railroad. The Association meets yearly on a Thursday night and continues its sessions until Saturday. An attendance of twelve hundred is usual. The best speakers in America address the Association, but its chief attractions are found in the enthusiastic local talent it has evoked. It is not simply educational in character, but literary, musical, and social as well. A co-operative work for rural-school uplift has given wholesome entertainment to a wide district, created a taste for literature in school and home, fostered the love of good music, and advanced every ideal of citizenship. Rural life has become sweeter, saner and satisfying.

But it is chiefly in such instrumentalities as the Amherst Movement that promise is found, inasmuch as this movement is based upon betterment of the fundamental characteristics of farm life and reaches after every ele-

16

ment in its crowning worth.   Just as Raiffeisen in Germany discovered that co-operative societies formed upon the principle of pure benevolence possessed no vitality, but that when organized as essentially business concerns upon a Christian and not a mercenary basis, they become effective, so this movement is grounded upon scientific agricultural education, while it confidently claims the co-operation and leadership of the church in higher tasks.   The movement has its centre at the Massachusetts Agricultural College at Amherst.   Kenyon L. Butterfield, President of the College, is its foremost exponent.   But the Amherst Movement is but an illustrative instance of a nation-wide impulse embracing every agency engaged in agricultural research, organization, and education, from the federal Department of Education down through the State departments and State colleges to the county societies, from the Farmers' National Congress to the local meeting of the Farmers' Institute, and embracing the Grange and the agricultural press, through all of whose extent two salient features emerge—a call for co-operation of all agencies and for the enlistment of the influence of the church.   Dr. Tallmadge Root of the Federal Council of the Churches says in regard to the Amherst Movement, " It is a great civic revival, deeply moral and religious in its essential meaning, whose immediate field is the country community and whose natural leader is the church."

The public school is contributing its quota, and a large one, to the solution of the recreative and social need.   Twelve States have enacted laws authorizing the appointment of recreative commissions and authorizing school boards to spend funds for social and recreative purposes.   In Kentucky a league of citizens raised funds by popular subscription for a model schoolhouse, adapted to community use. One county in Texas has issued bonds for half a million dollars to build five schools equipped as social centres. The United States Bureau of Education becomes a clearing-house of information on the movement, issuing bulletins on social and recreation work. It is proposed to add to the Federal Department of Education an expert on the activities in school buildings after school hours. The slogan of the movement is: " We are going to have a new rural life. The farm is not to have the life of a race of hermits."

And even Congress is found investigating the problem, proposing remedies, and making the same demand for leadership upon the church. In 1908 President Roosevelt appointed a Country Life Commission to report upon the condition of country life, the means available for supplying the deficiencies which exist, and the best methods of organized permanent effort along the lines of betterment of rural conditions. The Commission points out the need of four great forces: " Knowledge—the underlying facts must be understood "; " Education—there must be a new kind of education adapted to the real needs of the farming people "; " Organization—there must be a vast enlargement of voluntary organized effort among farmers "; and " Spiritual Forces—the forces and institutions that make for morality and spiritual ideals among rural people must be energized. We miss the heart of the problem if we neglect to foster personal character and neighborhood righteousness. The best way to preserve ideals for private conduct and public life is to build up the institutions of religion. The church has great power of leadership. The whole people should understand that it is vitally important to stand behind the rural church and to help it to become a great power in developing concrete country life ideals. It is especially important that the country church recognize that it has a social responsibility to the entire community as well as a religious responsibility to its own group of people. . . . Any consideration of the problem of rural life that leaves out of account the function and the possibilities of the church, and of related institutions, would be grossly inadequate. This is not only because in the last analysis the country life problem is a moral problem, or that in the best development of the individual the great motives and results are religious and spiritual, but because from the pure sociological point of view the church is fundamentally a necessary institution in country life. . . . This gives the rural church a position of peculiar difficulty, and one of unequalled opportunity. The time has arrived when the church must take a larger leadership, both as an institution and through its pastors, in the social reorganization of country life."*

It is manifest that there is a great movement in progress for rural betterment, and through movement and need alike, a great call to the church. In Canada that call is still more imperative. Our percentage of growth in population is greater than that of the United States; theirs was 21 per cent. in the past decade; ours 34. Our percentage of immigration is greater; 31.9 against their 11.5 per cent. The urbanization of population is more rapid with us; their percentage of rural population has

* Report of the Country Life Commission, pp. 17, 60.

fallen 5.8 per cent. in ten years, ours 8 per cent; in twenty years theirs has been lowered by 10.2, ours by 13.8. Instances of percentages of city growth with us are almost unequalled anywhere, Winnipeg, 221 per cent. in ten years, Edmonton 848, Calgary 893, Regina 1,243, Swift Current, 1,430, and Saskatoon, 10,523 per cent. in one decade. The development of corporation control over production and sources of wealth is with us perhaps the most riotously rapid the world has yet seen. Seven years ago trust control had scarce begun in Canada; already it dominates almost every one of the more lucrative sources of wealth. On the other hand the call is imperative because the church is as yet strong in Canada in the rural districts,—to act efficiently she must meet the situation before becoming weakened. And yet again, her allies are with us of the strongest. McGill University, through her faculty of agriculture in Macdonald College at Ste. Anne's, leads the world in university education for agriculture. Ontario alone employs over a hundred trained, skilled, competent agriculturists, teaching, and travelling over the Province furnishing information and advice upon farm conditions and possibilities. Dr. Robertson says: " In those regards Canada is in the front rank among all the nations of which I have any knowledge."* Such are the factors in the call to the church in Canada.

Life has two sovereign moments: one when man settles down
To some life-worthy purpose; one, when he gains the crown.†

* Conservation Commission III, p. 90.
† Matthew Richey Wright, in Rand's " Treasury of Canadian Verse."

The second of these sovereign movements is exemplified among us in the work of Dr. Grenfell, by which a population not indeed agricultural, and yet distinctly rural, has been uplifted economically and socially and spiritually to a new plane of life; the first opens before rural Canada to-day.

———————

An old farm-house with meadows wide
And sweet with clover on each side;
A bright-eyed boy, who looks from out
The door with woodbine wreathed about,
And wishes this one thought all day:
" Oh, if I could but fly away
   From this dull spot, the world to see,
  How happy, happy, happy,
   How happy I should be!"

Amid the city's constant din
A man who round the world has been,
Who, 'mid the tumult and the throng,
Is thinking, thinking, all day long:
" Oh, could I only tread once more
The field-path to the farm-house door,
   The old green meadow could I see,
  How happy, happy, happy,
   How happy I should be!"
          —Annie Douglas Robinson.

BIBLIOGRAPHY

Anderson, Wilbert L., LL.D., "The Country Town." Baker & Taylor Co., 1906. $1.00.

Ashenhurst, J. O., "The Day of the Country Church." Funk & Wagnalls, 1910. $1.00.

Beard, A. F., D.D., "The Story of John Frederick Oberlin." Pilgrim Press, 1909. $1.00.

Bayley, L. H., "The Country Life Movement." Macmillan Co., 1911. $1.25.

Butterfield, K. L., "The Country Church and the Rural Problem." University of Chicago Press, 1911. $1.00.

Butterfield, L. H., "Chapters in Rural Progress." University of Chicago Press, 1908. $1.00.

Carney, Mabel, "Country Life and the Country School." Row, Peterson & Co., 1912. $1.00.

Fiske, Walter, "The Challenge of the Country." The Association Press, 1913. 75c.

Gladden, Washington, D.D., "The Christian League of Connecticut." The Century Co., 1883.

Gladden, Washington, D.D., "Parish Problems." The Century Co., 1887. $1.50.

Hayward, C. E., "Institutional Work for the Country Church." Burlington Free Press Association, 1900. 50c.

McKeever, W. A., "Farm Boys and Girls." Macmillan Co., 1913. 75c.

Mott, John R., "The Future Leadership of the Church," Student Department, Y. M. C. A., 1909. $1.00.

Plunkett, Sir Horace, "The Rural Life Problem in the United States." Macmillan Co., 1911. $1.25.

Roads, Charles, D.D., "Rural Christendom." American Sunday School Union, 1910. 90c.

Robertson, James W., LL.D., "The Satisfaction of Country Life." Sturgis & Walton, 1913. $1.00.

Strong, Josiah, D.D., "The New Era." The Baker & Taylor Co., 1893. 75c.

Vincent, J. H., D.D., "The Modern Sunday School." Eaton & Mains, 1908. $1.00.

Wilson, Warren H., "The Church of the Open Country." Student Movement, 1911. 50c.

Wilson, Warren H., "The Evolution of the Country Community." Pilgrim Press, 1912. $1.00.

Annals of the American Academy of Social and Political Science. Philadelphia, March, 1912. $1.50.

Reports of the Commission of Conservation, Canada, for 1910, 1911, and 1912, Government Bureau, Ottawa.

Report of the Country Life Commission, United States. Sturgis & Walton, 1909. 75c.

"Messages of the Men and Religion Movement," Vol. VI, "The Rural Church." Association Press, 1912. $4.00 for set of seven volumes.

"Social Service," Edited by R. W. MacIntosh. R. Douglas Fraser, 1911. 50c.

"The Rural Church and Community Betterment." Report of Y. M. C. A. Conference. Association Press, 1911. 75c.

"The Country Church and Rural Progress." Report of Y. M. C. A. Conference. Association Press, 1912. 75c.

Six Pamphlets. "A Rural Survey in Pennsylvania," "— in Kentucky," "— in Missouri," "— in Tennesee," "— in Indiana," "— in Maryland." "Department of Church and Country Life.' 156 Fifth Avenue, New York.

"Rural Manhood," a magazine published by the Y. M. C. A. Association Press, 124 E. 28th Street, New York. $1.00 a year.